AI for Educators

Innovative Strategies and Solutions to Reduce
Stress and Burnout, Maximize Workload Efficiency,
Engage Learning and Elevate Classrooms with 125+
Time-Saving Prompts and Activities

Taylor Madison

Contents

Introduction

Welcome to your comprehensive guide designed to equip teachers, administrators, and educational professionals with the knowledge and skills necessary to harness the power of Artificial Intelligence (AI) in the educational landscape. As AI continues to reshape various sectors, its impact on education offers both exciting opportunities and unique challenges. This book aims to demystify AI for educators, providing clear explanations, practical applications, and interactive activities tailored to the needs of the educational community.

The incorporation of AI into educational settings is not just about leveraging new technologies; it's about enhancing teaching practices, improving student outcomes, and streamlining administrative tasks. However, the integration of AI in education requires more than just technical know-how—it demands a deep understanding of pedagogical principles, ethical considerations, and a commitment to continuous learning. This book is structured to guide you through these aspects in a logical, accessible manner.

Each chapter in this book follows a strategic format designed to build your AI literacy step by step. Starting with the basics of AI prompt crafting and moving through personalized learning, interactive classroom activities, critical thinking enhancements, assessment and feedback mechanisms, curriculum development, professional development, administrative tasks, and finally, building your AI toolkit, this book covers the spectrum of AI's educational applications.

In each chapter, you will find:

1. Clear Overviews and Objectives: Understand the focus of each section and what you can expect to learn, setting the stage for deeper exploration.

2. Key Concepts and Best Practices: Delve into essential ideas, strategies, and ethical guidelines necessary for effectively integrating AI into educational contexts.

3. Practical Activities: Engage in hands-on activities designed to apply what you've learned directly to your educational setting. Each activity includes specific AI generation prompts—these are questions or statements you can input into AI tools to generate useful content, insights, or data relevant to your teaching or administrative needs. These prompts are crafted to be immediately applicable, providing a bridge between theory and practice.

4. Post-Implementation Prompts: After implementing the activity, these prompts will guide you to reflect on the experience, evaluate the outcomes, and think critically about how the process can be improved or adapted for future use. These reflection exercises are vital for reinforcing learning and encouraging iterative improvement.

By integrating activities throughout each chapter, this book promotes active learning and practical application, ensuring that you're not just passively absorbing information but actively engaging with the material. The activities are designed to be adaptable to various educational levels and settings, encouraging customization to meet the specific needs of your students or administrative responsibilities.

Whether you're a seasoned educator familiar with AI concepts or a newcomer curious about the potential of artificial intelligence in education, this book offers a structured pathway to understanding and applying AI effectively. Let's embark on this journey together, exploring the transformative power of AI in shaping the future of education.

Chapter One

Basics of AI Prompt Crafting

1.1 Understanding the Structure of an Effective AI Prompt

In the rapidly evolving landscape of education, the integration of Artificial Intelligence (AI) has opened new avenues for enhancing teaching and learning. One of the fundamental skills that educators need to harness the full potential of AI in the classroom is the ability to craft effective AI prompts. Understanding the structure of an effective AI prompt is crucial for educators as it directly influences the quality and applicability of AI-generated content and responses.

AI prompts are not just questions or commands; they are the bridge between the educator's instructional needs and the AI's capability to provide relevant, accurate, and useful information or materials. An effective prompt leads to outcomes that are aligned with educational goals, whether it's creating personalized learning materials, generating assessments, or providing data analysis. Therefore, clarity, specificity, and intent become the cornerstones of a well-constructed AI prompt.

However, understanding and applying these elements can be challenging without a clear framework. This section is designed to demystify the process and provide educators with the knowledge and tools to create prompts that yield meaningful and educational outcomes. By breaking down the key components of successful AI prompts and guiding educators through practical activities, this section aims to build a solid foundation for integrating AI effectively into classroom instruction and curriculum design.

Remember that crafting AI prompts is both an art and a science. It requires a blend of clear communication, understanding of educational objectives, and familiarity with the AI's capabilities. With practice and reflection, educators can develop the skill to create prompts that leverage AI technology to enhance the educational experience and outcomes for their students.

Activity: Deconstructing an AI Prompt

Tools & Materials Needed:

- AI educational tool or platform.
- Sample AI prompts (provided in this activity).
- Computer with internet connection.
- Worksheet for notes (optional).

Time Needed: Approximately 30 minutes.

Outcome: An enhanced understanding of the components of effective AI prompts.

Instructions:

1. Prepare Your Workspace:
   - Choose a comfortable and quiet working area.
   - Open your AI educational tool on your computer.
   - Have your worksheet or a digital document ready for taking notes.

2. Analyze the Sample Prompt:
   - Review the following sample AI prompt: "Generate a quiz for 10th-grade biology covering photosynthesis."
   - Break down the prompt into its components: Clarity, Specificity, Intent, Context, and Desired Output.

3. Evaluate Clarity and Specificity:
   - Consider whether the prompt clearly states what is needed. Is there any ambiguity that could lead to an unexpected outcome?
   - Determine if the prompt includes specific details, such as the subject level (10th grade) and topic (photosynthesis).

4. Identify Intent and Context:
   - Reflect on the intent behind the prompt. What is the ultimate goal of generating this quiz?
   - Assess whether the prompt provides sufficient context for the AI to generate a relevant and accurate quiz.

5. Determine the Desired Output:
   - Specify what type of response is expected from the AI. In this case, it's a

quiz, but what format should it be in? How many questions should it include?

6. Refine the Prompt:

   ○ Based on your analysis, rewrite the prompt to enhance its clarity, specificity, intent, context, and desired output. For example, "Create a 15-question multiple-choice quiz for 10th-grade biology focusing on the process of photosynthesis and its importance."

7. Review and Reflect:

   ○ Compare the original and refined prompts. Note the differences and how the changes might affect the AI's response.

   ○ Reflect on how the exercise has changed your understanding of crafting effective AI prompts.

8. Additional Tips:

   ○ Practice with different prompts and subjects to improve your skills.

   ○ Share your refined prompts with colleagues to get feedback and new ideas.

   ○ Apply these principles when crafting your own AI prompts for classroom use.

1.2 Customizing AI Prompts for Educational Needs

Differentiation is key in education. Each student comes with unique backgrounds, learning styles, and abilities, requiring educators to adapt their teaching approaches. Similarly, AI prompts must be customized for different educational needs to be truly effective. This customization can range from altering prompts to better fit various subjects and grade levels to ensuring they meet specific learning objectives.

Furthermore, inclusivity and accessibility are paramount. AI prompts should be designed to accommodate all students, including those with special needs or those who learn differently. By considering these factors, educators can create a learning environment where all students have the opportunity to succeed.

Activity: Customizing AI Prompts for Classroom Scenarios

Tools & Materials Needed:

- AI prompt tool or platform

- List of generic AI prompts

- Curriculum guidelines for different subjects and grade levels

- Profiles of student learning styles and needs

Time Needed: 1 hour

Outcome: A set of customized AI prompts tailored to specific classroom scenarios, subjects, grade levels, and student needs.

Instructions:

1. Gather Your Resources:

   ○ Collect the list of generic AI prompts and curriculum guidelines for the subjects and grade levels you teach.

   ○ Review the profiles of different student learning styles and needs within your classroom.

2. Analyze the Generic Prompts:

   a. Choose one generic AI prompt from the list provided.

   b. Evaluate how well this prompt aligns with your curriculum guidelines and the needs of your students.

3. Customize for Differentiation:

   a. Modify the chosen AI prompt to better align with a specific subject and grade level. Consider the language complexity, subject-specific terms, and the depth of knowledge required.

   b. Create three variations of the prompt to cater to beginner, intermediate, and advanced students within that grade level.

4. Enhance for Inclusivity:

   ○ Adjust the modified prompts to ensure they are accessible and inclusive. This could involve simplifying language, providing additional context, or offering multiple ways to respond.

   ○ Consider the needs of students with disabilities, English language learners, and those with different learning styles.

5. Test and Reflect:

   ○ If possible, test your customized prompts with a small group of students or with a colleague.

   ○ Reflect on the effectiveness of the prompts and make any necessary adjustments based on feedback.

6. Share and Collaborate:

- ○ Share your customized prompts with colleagues teaching the same grade level or subject. Discuss how the prompts could be further adapted for different classroom scenarios.

- ○ Collect feedback and additional customization ideas to refine your prompts further.

By completing this activity, you will develop a deeper understanding of how to tailor AI prompts to meet the diverse needs of their students, enhancing the learning experience and ensuring that all students can benefit from AI-assisted education.

1.3 Crafting Your First AI Prompt

Creating your first AI prompt is an exciting step into the realm of AI-assisted education. This process begins with understanding your educational goals and the specific challenges you aim to address using AI. A well-crafted prompt serves as a clear, direct communication tool between you and the AI, guiding it to generate useful and relevant outputs. Whether you're looking to generate content, assess student understanding, or provide personalized learning experiences, the effectiveness of AI in your classroom starts with the quality of your prompts.

Getting started with AI prompt creation involves identifying the educational goals that matter most to you and your students. Consider what you wish to achieve with AI assistance: Do you need to generate quiz questions, create engaging lesson content, or perhaps offer personalized feedback? From there, prompt development involves translating these goals into clear, concise questions or statements that direct the AI towards the desired outcome.

Activity: Crafting Your First Educational AI Prompt

Tools & Materials Needed:

- AI prompt tool or educational AI platform access

- List of educational goals or challenges

- Notebook or digital document for note-taking

Time Needed: 30 minutes

Outcome: Your first customized AI prompt tailored to a specific educational goal or challenge.

Instructions:

1. Define Your Educational Goal:

○ Choose one educational goal or challenge from your list that you believe AI could help address. This could be anything from creating study materials to generating practice questions or providing student feedback.

2. Understand the AI's Capabilities:

○ Familiarize yourself with the AI tool or platform you are using. Understand what types of requests it can handle and the format it requires for prompts.

3. Draft Your Initial Prompt:

○ Based on your chosen educational goal and the AI's capabilities, draft an initial prompt. Keep it simple and direct, focusing clearly on what you want the AI to produce.

4. Refine Your Prompt:

○ Review the initial prompt and refine it for clarity and specificity. Ensure it is open-ended enough to generate useful content but specific enough to meet your educational goal. Consider adding context or constraints where necessary.

5. Test and Evaluate:

○ Input your refined prompt into the AI tool and evaluate the output. Does it meet your educational needs? Is it relevant and useful for your classroom?

6. Iterate and Improve:

○ Based on the AI's response, make adjustments to your prompt as needed. This may involve specifying the grade level, subject area, or type of response you are seeking. Test the revised prompt and evaluate the new output.

7. Document and Reflect:

○ Once satisfied with the AI-generated content, document your final prompt and the AI's response. Reflect on this process: What worked well? What challenges did you encounter? How can you apply this experience to future AI prompt creation?

By completing this activity, you will gain practical experience in crafting AI prompts and understand how to leverage AI tools effectively to meet educational objectives. This foundational skill is essential for integrating AI into teaching and learning processes, enabling you to customize and enhance their instructional strategies.

1.4 Refining and Evaluating AI Prompts

Creating an effective AI prompt is an iterative process. Just as educators continually assess and refine their teaching methods, AI prompts must also be regularly reviewed and updated to ensure they are meeting educational objectives effectively. This section will delve into the importance of establishing a feedback loop for continuous improvement of AI prompts, highlighting how student responses and outcomes can inform revisions. Understanding how to refine AI prompts based on feedback ensures that they remain relevant, engaging, and effective over time.

Testing AI-generated content in the classroom provides direct insights into the strengths and weaknesses of your prompts. Students' reactions, understanding, and engagement levels serve as valuable feedback. Incorporating this feedback into subsequent iterations of AI prompts can significantly enhance their quality and effectiveness. Additionally, this section will introduce quality checks and criteria for evaluating AI prompts, such as clarity, relevance, and alignment with learning objectives, which are crucial for maintaining high educational standards.

Activity: Refining AI Prompts for Classroom Use

Tools & Materials Needed:

- A set of initial AI prompts (provided or previously created)

- Student feedback on AI-generated content (real or hypothetical scenarios)

- Criteria checklist for evaluating AI prompts

- Notebook or digital document for recording revisions

Time Needed: 45 minutes

Outcome: A refined set of AI prompts optimized based on feedback and quality checks.

Instructions:

1. Gather Initial Prompts and Feedback:

    ○ Start with a set of AI prompts that have been used in the classroom or hypothetical scenarios. Collect any available student feedback on the content generated from these prompts or imagine potential student responses based on your understanding of your students.

2. Review Feedback and Identify Themes:

    ○ Analyze the student feedback for common themes or issues. Note any recurring misunderstandings, questions, or engagement issues related to the AI-generated content.

3. Apply Quality Checks:

○ Use the provided criteria checklist to evaluate each AI prompt. Assess factors such as clarity, relevance to learning objectives, student engagement potential, and inclusivity.

4. Revise Prompts Based on Feedback:

○ Refine each AI prompt based on the student feedback and quality checks. Make adjustments to clarify, specify, or realign the prompts with educational goals. Aim to address any misunderstandings or engagement issues highlighted by the feedback.

5. Test and Collect New Feedback:

○ If possible, apply the revised prompts in your classroom and collect new student feedback. If not, consider how students might respond based on your revisions and past experiences.

6. Iterate the Refinement Process:

○ Review the new feedback and further refine the prompts as necessary. This may involve additional adjustments for clarity, engagement, or alignment with educational objectives.

7. Document and Reflect:

○ Record the final versions of your AI prompts and note any changes made during the refinement process. Reflect on how the feedback and quality checks informed your revisions and consider how this iterative process can be applied to future AI prompt development.

Through this activity, you will learn the value of iterative refinement and feedback in crafting effective AI prompts. By continually evaluating and adjusting AI prompts, you can ensure that you are leveraging AI tools to their fullest potential, thereby enhancing the learning experience for your students.

1.5 Practical Applications and Examples

Integrating AI into educational practices is not just about understanding the theoretical aspects; it's also about seeing how these concepts play out in real-world scenarios. This section explores practical applications and examples of AI prompts in various educational settings. By examining case studies and real-life examples, educators can gain insights into how AI prompts are being used to enhance teaching and learning, identify common challenges, and discover innovative solutions.

Furthermore, the collaborative development of AI prompts can significantly enhance their effectiveness and applicability. When educators come together to share ideas and experiences, they can refine their prompts to be more inclusive, engaging, and aligned with educational objectives. This collaborative process not only improves the quality of AI prompts but also fosters a community of practice among educators, encouraging ongoing learning and professional development.

Activity 1: Creating Interactive History Lessons

Tools & Materials Needed:

- AI educational tool or platform

- Access to digital archives or history databases

- Standard history curriculum topics for the intended grade level

Time Needed: 45 minutes

Outcome: A set of interactive, AI-generated history lesson prompts that encourage critical thinking and engagement.

Instructions:

1. Select a Historical Topic:

   ○ Choose a specific event or period from your history curriculum, such as the American Revolution or Ancient Egyptian civilization.

2. Draft Initial AI Prompts:

   ○ Craft AI prompts aimed at generating engaging content related to your selected topic. For example: "Generate a dialogue between two opposing figures during the American Revolution discussing their viewpoints."

3. Input AI Prompts:

   ○ Enter your drafted AI prompts into the AI educational tool. Evaluate the generated content for historical accuracy and engagement level.

4. Create Interactive Activities:

   ○ Use the AI-generated content to create interactive activities. For example, if the AI created a dialogue, have students perform a role-play based on it. Alternatively, if the AI provided an overview of Ancient Egypt, develop a virtual scavenger hunt where students find artifacts related to the era.

5. Feedback and Revision:

   ○ Test these activities in your classroom and collect student feedback. Use this feedback to refine your AI prompts and activities, focusing on increasing engagement and understanding.

Activity 2: Developing Math Problem-Solving Skills

Tools & Materials Needed:

- AI educational tool or platform

- List of math topics from the current curriculum

- Criteria for effective math problems (e.g., clarity, relevance to topic, appropriate difficulty)

Time Needed: 1 hour

Outcome: A collection of AI-generated math problems tailored to different student skill levels, encouraging problem-solving and critical thinking.

Instructions:

1. Choose a Math Topic:

   ○ Select a math topic your students are currently learning, such as algebraic expressions or geometric shapes.

2. Craft AI Prompts for Problem Generation:

   ○ Create specific AI prompts to generate problems related to your chosen topic. For example: "Create five algebraic expression problems that challenge students to apply the distributive property."

3. Generate and Review Problems:

   ○ Input your AI prompts into the educational tool and review the generated math problems. Ensure they align with your curriculum and meet the established criteria.

4. Differentiate Problems:

   ○ Modify your AI prompts to generate problems at varying difficulty levels. For instance, add "for beginners" or "for advanced learners" to tailor the complexity of the problems.

5. Classroom Implementation and Feedback:

   ○ Introduce the AI-generated problems to your students in a suitable format, such as a worksheet or digital platform. After completion, gather student feedback on the problems' clarity and difficulty.

6. Refine and Expand:

   ○ Based on student feedback, refine your AI prompts and generate additional problems. Aim to cover a wider range of topics and difficulty levels for comprehensive practice.

Activity 3: Enhancing Language Arts with Creative Writing

Tools & Materials Needed:

* AI educational tool or platform

* List of literary genres or themes (e.g., mystery, adventure, friendship)

* Rubric for evaluating creative writing (focusing on creativity, coherence, grammar, and engagement)

Time Needed: 1 hour

Outcome: A series of AI-generated creative writing prompts that stimulate imagination and improve writing skills.

Instructions:

1. Select a Theme or Genre:

   ○ Pick a theme or genre for the creative writing assignment, such as science fiction or personal narrative.

2. Develop AI Prompts:

   ○ Formulate AI prompts to generate creative writing starters or scenarios. For example: "Generate a science fiction story starter set in a future where water is the most valuable resource."

3. Generate Writing Starters:

   ○ Use the AI tool to generate writing starters or scenarios based on your prompts. Review them for creativity and potential to engage students.

4. Classroom Application:

   ○ Assign the AI-generated starters to your students for a creative writing activity. Provide them with the writing rubric and specific guidelines (e.g., word count, key elements to include).

5. Peer Review and Revision:

   ○ Organize a peer review session where students exchange their writings and provide feedback based on the rubric. Encourage constructive criticism and suggestions for improvement.

6. Reflect and Adapt:

- ○ Collect student writings and feedback. Reflect on the effectiveness of the AI-generated prompts and student engagement. Adjust future prompts based on observations and student suggestions to better meet their creative and educational needs.

Chapter Two

Prompts for Personalized Learning

2.1 Assessing Individual Learning Styles and Needs

Understanding each student's unique learning style and educational needs is essential for effective teaching. By identifying how each student best absorbs, processes, and retains information, educators can tailor their instruction to better suit individual preferences, thereby enhancing learning outcomes. AI can play a crucial role in this process by providing tools to assess and analyze students' learning styles and needs efficiently.

Crafting AI prompts for this purpose involves asking the right questions and setting up scenarios that reveal students' preferences, whether they are visual, auditory, kinesthetic, or read/write learners. By employing AI-driven quizzes, surveys, and interactive activities, educators can gather valuable data on their students, leading to more personalized and effective teaching strategies.

Activity 1: Creating a Learning Style AI Survey

Tools & Materials Needed:

- AI educational tool or survey platform
- List of questions pertaining to learning styles
- Computer or tablet with internet access

Time Needed: 30 minutes to create, 15 minutes for students to complete

Outcome: A comprehensive understanding of each student's preferred learning style.

Instructions:

1. Draft AI Prompts for Survey Questions:

   ○ Develop specific AI prompts such as "Create survey questions to determine if a student prefers visual, auditory, reading/writing, or kinesthetic learning styles."

2. Create the Survey:

   ○ Input the AI prompt into your chosen AI tool or survey platform to generate questions. Incorporate these questions into a learning style survey.

3. Administer the Survey:

   ○ Distribute the survey to students and allow time for completion. Encourage honesty for the most accurate results.

4. Analyze Results:

   ○ Review responses to understand each student's learning style. Note trends and preferences.

5. Adapt Teaching Strategies:

   ○ Tailor your teaching methods based on the survey results to better accommodate different learning styles.

Activity 2: Interactive Learning Style Discovery Session

Tools & Materials Needed:

- Various learning materials (videos, articles, objects, diagrams)

- AI tool for generating activity scenarios

- Classroom space for different activity stations

Time Needed: 1 hour

Outcome: Hands-on insights into students' preferred learning modalities.

Instructions:

1. Prepare Materials:

   ○ Set up different stations in the classroom, each representing a distinct learning style.

2. Craft AI Activity Prompts:

   ○ Use the AI tool with the prompt: "Generate activities that explain the concept of the water cycle tailored to visual, auditory, reading/writing, and kinesthetic learners."

3. Conduct the Session:

   ○ Students rotate through stations, engaging with the activities. Observe their interactions and preferences.

4. Gather Feedback:

   ○ Ask students which station they found most engaging and why.

5. Evaluate and Plan:

   ○ Use the feedback to identify learning styles and adapt future lessons accordingly.

Activity 3: AI-Assisted Reflective Journaling

Tools & Materials Needed:

- Digital journal platform or physical notebooks

- AI tool for generating reflective questions

- Guidelines for reflective journaling

Time Needed: Ongoing; allocate 15-20 minutes per journal entry

Outcome: Insights into students' self-perceived learning styles and educational needs.

Instructions:

1. Set Up Journaling Framework:

   ○ Explain the concept and benefits of reflective journaling to students, providing clear guidelines.

2. Generate Reflective Prompts:

   ○ Use the AI tool with prompts like "Generate reflective questions that help students analyze their learning preferences and challenges."

3. Implement Regular Journaling:

   ○ Schedule regular sessions for students to write in their journals, responding to the AI-generated prompts.

4. Review and Discuss:

- With permission, review entries to gather insights into learning preferences and discuss these with students to validate findings.

5. Adapt and Personalize:

- Tailor instruction based on journal insights to better meet students' learning needs.

2.2 Creating Personalized Learning Paths

Personalized learning paths represent a transformative approach in education, tailoring instruction to meet the unique needs, skills, and interests of each student. By leveraging AI, educators can develop customized learning plans that not only address individual learning styles and paces but also accommodate specific strengths and areas for improvement. This strategic approach fosters a more engaging, effective, and student-centered educational experience.

Utilizing AI to create personalized learning paths involves gathering data on student performance and preferences, then translating this information into actionable teaching strategies. AI can help generate lesson plans, study materials, and activities that align with each student's profile, thereby maximizing their learning potential. Below are activities designed to guide educators through the process of using AI to craft personalized learning paths for their students.

Activity 1: Designing a Customized Lesson Plan

Tools & Materials Needed:

- AI educational tool or platform

- Student performance data and learning style information

- Access to curriculum standards and resources

Time Needed: 1 hour

Outcome: A detailed, AI-generated lesson plan customized for a hypothetical student's needs and learning style.

Instructions:

1. Collect Student Data:

- Compile information on a hypothetical student's learning style, performance data, and areas of interest.

2. Generate Lesson Plan Outline:

- Use the AI tool with the prompt: "Create a lesson plan outline for a [specific subject and grade level] student with [specify learning style] who needs improvement in [specific area]. Include objectives, activities, and resources."

3. Customize Lesson Activities:

   ○ Input into the AI tool: "Generate interactive activities that cater to a [specify learning style] student focusing on [specific area of improvement]."

4. Compile and Review:

   ○ Combine the AI-generated outline and activities into a complete lesson plan. Review and adjust as necessary to ensure alignment with curriculum standards and student needs.

5. Feedback and Iteration:

   ○ Imagine student feedback or consult with colleagues to refine the lesson plan further.

Activity 2: Creating Personalized Study Materials

Tools & Materials Needed:

- AI educational tool or content generator

- Information on individual student needs and preferences

- Digital or physical formats for study materials

Time Needed: 45 minutes

Outcome: Tailored study materials designed to match an individual student's learning preferences and requirements.

Instructions:

1. Identify Learning Goals:

   ○ Determine specific learning goals based on the hypothetical student's needs and curriculum requirements.

2. Generate Study Materials:

   ○ Enter into the AI tool: "Develop study materials focused on [specific topic] for a student with [specific learning style and needs], ensuring content is engaging and informative."

3. Review and Customize:

- Review the AI-generated materials for accuracy and appropriateness. Make any necessary adjustments to better suit the student's learning style and needs.

4. Implementation and Feedback:

- Envision implementing these materials with the student and receiving feedback. Use this hypothetical feedback to make final adjustments.

Activity 3: Planning an AI-Assisted Personalized Assessment

Tools & Materials Needed:

- AI educational tool or platform

- Details of the hypothetical student's learning progress and style

- Assessment standards and criteria

Time Needed: 1 hour

Outcome: A personalized assessment plan that evaluates the hypothetical student's understanding and mastery of the subject matter.

Instructions:

1. Define Assessment Objectives:

- Outline clear objectives for the assessment, based on the student's learning goals and areas requiring evaluation.

2. Craft AI Assessment Prompts:

- Use the prompt in the AI tool: "Create a set of assessment questions tailored for a student proficient in [subject] but struggling with [specific topic], accommodating a [specific learning style]."

3. Generate and Review Assessment:

- Use the AI-generated questions to construct a complete assessment. Review for alignment with learning objectives and student needs.

4. Refine Based on Hypothetical Feedback:

- Consider potential student responses and areas of confusion. Refine the assessment accordingly to ensure clarity and effectiveness.

By completing these activities, educators can practice using AI to create personalized educational experiences, leading to more targeted and effective teaching strategies that address the diverse needs of their students.

2.3 Enhancing Engagement through Personalization

Engagement is a critical component of effective learning. When students are engaged, they are more likely to absorb information, think critically, and apply what they have learned. Personalized learning, which tailors education to fit each student's strengths, needs, interests, and cultural background, significantly boosts engagement and motivation. By leveraging AI, educators can develop prompts that adapt lesson content and delivery to match students' unique interests and engagement levels, making learning more relevant and exciting.

Developing AI prompts for personalization involves understanding the diverse interests and learning styles within a classroom and using this knowledge to create dynamic, adaptable content. This approach not only supports individual learning paths but also encourages active participation and engagement among all students.

Activity 1: Tailoring Content to Student Interests

Tools & Materials Needed:

- AI educational tool or platform

- List of student interests and recent performance metrics

- Access to digital content resources

Time Needed: 1 hour

Outcome: Lesson content tailored to the interests and needs of the class, aiming to boost engagement.

Instructions:

1. Gather Data on Student Interests:

   ○ Compile a list of student interests, hobbies, and favorite subjects.

2. Develop AI Prompts:

   ○ Create specific AI prompts, such as "Generate a math problem set incorporating soccer for students interested in sports" or "Create a science lesson plan that relates photosynthesis to gardening."

3. Generate and Integrate Content:

   ○ Input your AI prompts into the educational tool to generate customized content. Review the content for suitability and alignment with curriculum goals.

4. Implement and Assess Engagement:

- Introduce the tailored content in your classroom. Observe and note changes in student engagement and participation.

5. Gather Feedback and Refine:

- Collect student feedback on the lesson. Use this feedback to refine future AI prompts and content personalization.

Activity 2: Adapting Presentation Styles

Tools & Materials Needed:

- AI educational tool or platform

- Information on students' preferred learning and presentation styles

- Multimedia resources (images, videos, text, audio)

Time Needed: 1 hour

Outcome: Multiple versions of the same lesson content, each adapted to different presentation styles.

Instructions:

1. Identify Presentation Preferences:

- Determine the preferred presentation styles of your students (visual, auditory, textual, kinesthetic).

2. Formulate AI Prompts:

- Write AI prompts tailored to these preferences, such as "Convert this traditional text-based history lesson into a visual infographic for visual learners" or "Create an audio narration of this chemistry lesson for auditory learners."

3. Create Diverse Content:

- Use the AI tool to generate content based on your prompts. Ensure each piece aligns with the original lesson objectives.

4. Deliver and Evaluate:

- Present the different versions of the content to corresponding student groups. Assess which formats yield the highest engagement and understanding.

5. Collect and Apply Feedback:

- ○ Ask students for feedback on the presentation style and its impact on their learning. Use this information to further personalize future lessons.

Activity 3: Personalizing Homework Assignments

Tools & Materials Needed:

- AI educational tool or content generator
- Student profiles detailing individual learning goals and challenges
- Digital or paper format for distributing assignments

Time Needed: 45 minutes

Outcome: Personalized homework assignments that cater to the unique learning needs and interests of each student.

Instructions:

1. Compile Individual Learning Profiles:

- ○ Summarize each student's learning goals, challenges, and interests.

2. Craft AI Prompts for Homework:

- ○ Develop AI prompts like "Design a set of personalized homework questions for a student struggling with fractions but interested in music" or "Create a short story writing assignment for a student interested in space exploration."

3. Generate Personalized Assignments:

- ○ Input your prompts into the AI tool to create customized homework assignments tailored to each student's profile.

4. Distribute and Monitor:

- ○ Hand out the personalized assignments. Monitor completion rates and student feedback to gauge effectiveness.

5. Review and Adapt:

- ○ Evaluate the success of the personalized homework in meeting individual learning needs. Adjust the approach based on student performance and feedback for future assignments.

These activities encourage educators to harness the power of AI in creating a more personalized, engaging learning experience for their students, thereby promoting greater involvement and better educational outcomes.

2.4 Addressing Challenges in Personalized Learning

Implementing personalized learning in the classroom comes with its set of challenges. Educators often face hurdles such as limited resources, diverse student needs, large class sizes, and varying levels of technological access. However, these obstacles can be managed and often overcome with thoughtful strategies and the aid of AI. By identifying common challenges and employing AI to develop targeted solutions, educators can create more inclusive, effective personalized learning environments.

Solution-based AI prompts can be a key tool in this process. These prompts help educators leverage AI to generate ideas, resources, and strategies tailored to specific classroom challenges. Whether it's finding ways to differentiate instruction effectively, managing large groups while attending to individual needs, or incorporating diverse resources to meet varied learning styles, AI can provide practical support and innovative solutions.

Activity 1: Optimizing Group Learning with AI

Tools & Materials Needed:

- AI educational tool or platform

- Details about class size, group dynamics, and individual student needs

- Access to digital collaboration tools

Time Needed: 1 hour

Outcome: A strategic plan for group learning activities tailored to diverse needs and class dynamics, enhanced by AI-generated solutions.

Instructions:

1. Identify Group Learning Challenges:

    ◦ List specific issues you face in implementing effective group learning in your classroom.

2. Generate AI Prompts:

    ◦ Create AI prompts addressing these challenges, such as "Generate strategies for managing diverse learning needs in large group settings" or "Suggest digital tools that facilitate collaborative learning for students with varying skill levels."

3. Implement AI Solutions:

  ○ Input your prompts into the AI educational tool and review the generated suggestions. Select the most feasible and relevant solutions.

4. Plan Group Activities:

  ○ Based on AI suggestions, plan group learning activities that cater to the needs of different students. Ensure each activity aligns with learning objectives and student interests.

5. Test and Reflect:

  ○ Implement the activities in your classroom. Afterwards, reflect on their effectiveness and gather student feedback for future improvements.

Activity 2: Integrating Supplemental Resources via AI

Tools & Materials Needed:

- AI educational tool or content generator

- Information on specific student learning gaps or interests

- List of available educational resources (online platforms, libraries, etc.)

Time Needed: 45 minutes

Outcome: A curated list of AI-recommended supplemental resources tailored to individual student needs.

Instructions:

1. Compile Learning Gaps and Interests:

  ○ Document distinct areas where students need additional support or express keen interest.

2. Develop AI Prompts for Resources:

  ○ Formulate prompts like "Identify supplemental resources for students struggling with algebraic concepts" or "Find engaging science experiments for kinesthetic learners interested in physics."

3. Curate Educational Materials:

  ○ Input the prompts into the AI tool to generate a list of resources. Review and select the most appropriate materials for your students.

4. Distribute and Monitor Use:

○ Share the resources with students, providing guidance on how to use them effectively. Monitor their engagement and progress.

5. Evaluate and Adjust:

○ Assess the impact of these resources on student learning. Adjust your approach based on feedback and results.

Activity 3: Personalizing Learning with Limited Tech Access

Tools & Materials Needed:

- AI tool accessible via basic technology (such as a smartphone or library computer)

- Details of students' access to technology at home and in school

- Traditional and digital teaching materials

Time Needed: 1 hour

Outcome: A personalized learning plan that accommodates students' varied levels of technology access.

Instructions:

1. Assess Tech Availability:

○ Survey the level of technology access available to your students both at home and in school.

2. Formulate AI Prompts for Low-Tech Solutions:

○ Write prompts such as "Provide personalized learning strategies for students with limited technology access" or "Suggest engaging offline activities that support personalized learning goals."

3. Generate and Implement Solutions:

○ Use the AI tool to generate ideas and strategies. Implement these solutions, blending traditional and digital methods to accommodate all students.

4. Monitor and Gather Feedback:

○ Observe student engagement and progress. Collect feedback to understand the effectiveness of the blended approach.

5. Refine and Adapt:

○ Based on observations and feedback, refine your personalized learning plans to better suit students' tech access and learning needs.

Through these activities, educators can navigate the complexities of personalized learning, utilizing AI to overcome common challenges and enhance educational experiences for all students.

2.5 Continuous Improvement and Adaptation

The journey toward effective personalized learning is ongoing and iterative. It is essential to continually refine approaches based on student feedback, performance data, and evolving educational goals. This process of continuous improvement ensures that personalized learning strategies remain relevant, engaging, and effective over time. Utilizing AI, educators can streamline this process by generating tools like surveys and feedback forms that help in collecting and analyzing student feedback efficiently.

Incorporating feedback-oriented AI prompts allows educators to craft specific questions and prompts that elicit meaningful insights from students. These insights can then inform the ongoing adaptation and refinement of personalized learning paths. By fostering an environment where feedback is regularly sought, analyzed, and acted upon, educators can create a dynamic learning experience that grows and evolves in tandem with their students' needs.

Activity 1: Creating and Implementing an AI-Generated Feedback Survey

Tools & Materials Needed:

- AI educational tool or survey platform

- Access to digital device and internet

- List of learning objectives and strategies currently employed

Time Needed: 1 hour for creation, variable for implementation and analysis

Outcome: Actionable student feedback on personalized learning strategies, informing future adaptations.

Instructions:

1. Identify Focus Areas:

○ Determine specific areas within your personalized learning strategy that you wish to evaluate, such as engagement, understanding, or material relevance.

2. Craft AI Prompts for Survey Creation:

○ Use prompts such as "Generate questions to assess student engagement with personalized learning materials" or "Create survey questions to evaluate student understanding in the latest unit."

3. Generate and Review the Survey:

○ Input your AI prompts into the educational tool to create the survey. Review and refine the questions to ensure they are clear and targeted.

4. Distribute and Collect Responses:

○ Share the survey with your students, providing instructions and a deadline for completion. Encourage honesty to gain valuable insights.

5. Analyze Feedback and Plan Adaptations:

○ Analyze the collected feedback to identify trends, successes, and areas for improvement. Plan specific adaptations to your personalized learning approach based on this analysis.

6. Post-Implementation AI Prompt for Educators:

○ "Analyze student survey responses to identify common themes and suggestions for enhancing personalized learning strategies."

Activity 2: Student Reflection Sessions Using AI-Prompted Questions

Tools & Materials Needed:

- AI tool for generating reflective questions

- Classroom set-up for small group discussions or individual reflection sessions

- Recording method (notebook, digital document, voice recorder)

Time Needed: 30-45 minutes

Outcome: In-depth understanding of student experiences and needs for refining personalized learning paths.

Instructions:

1. Formulate Reflective AI Prompts:

○ Create prompts such as "Generate reflective questions for students to assess their own progress and challenges in the current personalized learning path."

2. Conduct Reflection Sessions:

- Use the AI-generated questions to facilitate reflection sessions, either in small groups or individually. Record key insights and feedback.

3. Review and Identify Action Points:

- Analyze the reflections to identify common challenges, preferences, and suggestions for improvement.

4. Implement Changes and Communicate:

- Make necessary changes to the personalized learning strategies based on student feedback. Communicate these changes and the rationale behind them to your students.

Activity 3: Iterative Lesson Plan Revision with AI Assistance

Tools & Materials Needed:

- AI educational tool or lesson planner

- Student performance data and previous lesson plans

- Feedback collection tools (survey, direct feedback, observation notes)

Time Needed: 1-2 hours for revision and planning

Outcome: A revised lesson plan that incorporates student feedback and performance data for enhanced personalized learning.

Instructions:

1. Collect and Analyze Data:

- Gather recent student performance data and feedback on previous lessons. Identify key areas for improvement.

2. Develop AI Prompts for Lesson Revision:

- Construct prompts like "Suggest modifications for a lesson plan on [topic] based on student feedback indicating a need for more interactive activities" or "Revise a lesson plan to better suit the learning styles of students who performed below expectations in the last assessment."

3. Revise and Implement the Lesson Plan:

- Use the AI-generated suggestions to revise your lesson plan. Implement the revised plan in your classroom.

4. Collect Post-Lesson Feedback:

  ○ After teaching the revised lesson, collect student feedback to gauge the effectiveness of the changes.

5. Review and Plan Next Steps:

  ○ Analyze the post-lesson feedback. Determine further revisions or continue the cycle of feedback and adaptation for continuous improvement.

6. Post-Implementation AI Prompt for Educators:

  ○ "Generate a follow-up survey to evaluate the changes made to the lesson plan based on previous student feedback."

By engaging in these activities, educators can harness the power of AI to support the continuous improvement and adaptation of personalized learning strategies, ensuring they meet the evolving needs of their students.

Chapter Three

Prompts for Interactive Classroom Activities

3.1 Generating Engaging Content

Engaging content is the cornerstone of effective teaching and learning. It captures students' interest, motivates them to learn, and helps them understand and retain information. With the advent of AI, educators now have the tools to create content that is not only interesting and relevant but also tailored to the grade level and learning objectives of their students. By crafting AI prompts that generate compelling educational materials, educators can enhance the learning experience and outcomes for all students.

Creating AI prompts requires a clear understanding of the subject matter, the educational goals, and the interests and needs of the students. These prompts should be designed to produce content that is engaging, informative, and aligned with curriculum standards. This innovative approach allows educators to supplement traditional teaching methods with dynamic content that resonates with today's learners.

Activity 1: Creating AI-Generated Short Stories for Reading Comprehension

Tools & Materials Needed:

- AI content generation tool or platform

- Curriculum standards for language arts

- Criteria for evaluating reading comprehension materials

Time Needed: 1 hour

Outcome: A set of engaging AI-generated short stories tailored to students' grade level and interests.

Instructions:

1. Identify Key Themes and Interests:

   ○ Determine themes or topics that resonate with your students and align with language arts curriculum standards.

2. Craft AI Prompts for Story Generation:

   ○ Develop specific AI prompts, such as "Generate a short story for [grade level] students, themed around [chosen theme], that includes a moral lesson and vocabulary words from unit [specific unit or topic]."

3. Generate and Review Stories:

   ○ Input the prompts into the AI tool to create short stories. Review the stories to ensure they meet educational standards and engage students.

4. Implement and Assess Engagement:

   ○ Use the AI-generated stories in reading comprehension activities. Observe student engagement and comprehension levels.

5. Gather Feedback and Refine:

   ○ Collect student feedback on the stories. Use this feedback to refine future AI prompts and story content.

6. Post-Implementation AI Prompt for Educators:

   ○ "Analyze student feedback and engagement levels with AI-generated short stories to identify themes and elements that most effectively enhance reading comprehension for [grade level] students."

Activity 2: Developing AI-Generated Science Experiments

Tools & Materials Needed:

- AI educational tool or science content generator

- List of science curriculum topics and objectives

- Laboratory materials or virtual lab platform

Time Needed: 1-2 hours

Outcome: A collection of AI-generated science experiments tailored to curriculum topics and student interests.

Instructions:

1. Select Curriculum Topics:

   - Choose specific science topics from your curriculum that would benefit from hands-on experiments.

2. Formulate AI Prompts for Experiments:

   - Write AI prompts like "Create a detailed experiment plan for [grade level] students that demonstrates the principle of [chosen topic], including a hypothesis, materials list, and step-by-step instructions."

3. Generate and Adapt Experiments:

   - Use the AI tool to generate experiment plans. Adapt these plans as necessary to fit your classroom resources and student safety guidelines.

4. Conduct and Evaluate:

   - Implement the experiments in class. Evaluate student engagement, understanding, and scientific inquiry skills.

5. Collect Feedback and Improve:

   - Gather student feedback on the experiments. Refine future AI prompts based on this feedback and observed outcomes.

Activity 3: Crafting AI-Generated Historical Case Studies

Tools & Materials Needed:

- AI educational tool or platform

- History curriculum topics and learning objectives

- Evaluation criteria for historical understanding

Time Needed: 1 hour

Outcome: Engaging, AI-generated historical case studies that foster critical thinking and historical inquiry.

Instructions:

1. Identify Historical Topics:

  ○ Select historical topics or events relevant to your curriculum that would benefit from deeper analysis.

2. Develop AI Prompts for Case Studies:

  ○ Create AI prompts, such as "Generate a comprehensive case study for [grade level] students on [historical event], including background information, key figures, and discussion questions."

3. Generate and Review Case Studies:

  ○ Input your prompts into the AI tool. Review the generated case studies for accuracy, relevance, and engagement potential.

4. Implement in Classroom:

  ○ Use the case studies in classroom discussions, activities, or assessments. Monitor student engagement and historical understanding.

5. Gather Feedback and Refine:

  ○ Collect student feedback on the case studies. Use this information to improve future AI prompts and case study content.

By implementing these activities, educators can leverage AI to create a variety of engaging, curriculum-aligned content that caters to the diverse interests and needs of their students, thereby enhancing overall class engagement and learning outcomes.

3.2 Stimulating Classroom Discussions

Classroom discussions are a vital component of the learning process, promoting critical thinking, enhancing understanding, and encouraging active engagement among students. Effective discussions are driven by thought-provoking questions and topics that challenge students to think deeply, articulate their ideas, and engage with different perspectives. In this digital age, AI can be an invaluable tool in generating such stimulating discussion questions or topics that are relevant to the current lesson plans and aligned with educational goals.

Utilizing AI to craft discussion prompts can help educators diversify the subjects of conversation, ensuring that all students find something that resonates with them or sparks their interest. By providing examples of AI prompts for generating discussion questions, educators can seamlessly integrate this technology into their teaching strategy, fostering a dynamic and interactive classroom environment.

Activity 1: AI-Generated Discussion Questions for Literary Analysis

Tools & Materials Needed:

- AI educational tool or platform
- Text of a literary work or excerpt being studied
- Criteria for effective discussion questions

Time Needed: 30 minutes

Outcome: A list of AI-generated discussion questions tailored to a literary work, designed to deepen understanding and promote analysis.

Instructions:

1. Select a Literary Text:

   o Choose a novel, poem, or play that the class is currently studying.

2. Craft AI Prompts for Discussion Questions:

   o Create specific AI prompts such as "Generate in-depth discussion questions for [title of the work] that explore the themes of [specific themes]."

3. Generate and Review Questions:

   o Input your AI prompts into the educational tool to create a set of discussion questions. Review and select the most thought-provoking questions that align with your lesson objectives.

4. Facilitate Classroom Discussion:

   o Use the AI-generated questions to guide a classroom discussion on the literary work. Encourage students to provide evidence from the text to support their responses.

5. Evaluate and Reflect:

   o Observe student engagement and the depth of the discussion. Collect feedback from students on the discussion process.

6. Post-Implementation AI Prompt for Educators:

   o "Analyze the effectiveness of AI-generated discussion questions in promoting critical thinking and student engagement during literary analysis."

Activity 2: Developing Historical Inquiry with AI Prompts

Tools & Materials Needed:

- AI educational tool or platform

- Historical event or era from the curriculum

- Guidelines for historical inquiry and discussion

Time Needed: 45 minutes

Outcome: A comprehensive set of AI-generated questions designed to facilitate a deep inquiry into a historical event or era.

Instructions:

1. Identify a Historical Focus:

   ○ Select a specific event or era covered in your history curriculum.

2. Formulate AI Prompts for Inquiry Questions:

   ○ Write AI prompts like "Create questions that encourage deep inquiry into the causes and consequences of [historical event/era]."

3. Generate and Select Inquiry Questions:

   ○ Use the AI tool to generate a list of inquiry questions. Select questions that cover different aspects and perspectives of the historical topic.

4. Conduct the Historical Discussion:

   ○ Organize a class discussion using the AI-generated questions. Encourage students to use historical evidence and different perspectives in their answers.

5. Assess Student Engagement and Understanding:

   ○ Monitor the discussion for student engagement and the depth of understanding demonstrated. Gather feedback on the effectiveness of the questions.

Activity 3: AI-Enhanced Science Topic Debates

Tools & Materials Needed:

- AI educational tool or platform

- Current science curriculum topics

- Format and rules for classroom debates

Time Needed: 1 hour

Outcome: An engaging classroom debate on a science topic, facilitated by AI-generated questions and scenarios.

Instructions:

1. Choose a Science Topic:

   ○ Pick a controversial or debatable topic from your current science curriculum.

2. Create AI Prompts for Debate Questions:

   ○ Develop AI prompts such as "Generate debate questions and scenarios related to [science topic] that consider ethical, environmental, and technological viewpoints."

3. Generate Debate Content:

   ○ Input your prompts into the AI tool and compile the generated questions and scenarios for the debate.

4. Organize and Conduct the Debate:

   ○ Divide the class into teams or pairs and assign positions based on the AI-generated scenarios. Facilitate the debate, ensuring all students have the opportunity to contribute.

5. Evaluate and Debrief:

   ○ After the debate, discuss with students the different arguments and perspectives presented. Collect feedback on the learning experience and the effectiveness of the AI-generated content.

By incorporating these activities, educators can leverage AI to enrich classroom discussions, enhance student engagement, and deepen understanding of various subjects. These AI-generated prompts provide a starting point for dynamic and meaningful classroom interactions, driving critical thinking and collaborative learning.

3.3 Creating Interactive Games and Simulations

The incorporation of games and simulations into educational settings represents a dynamic shift towards more interactive and engaging learning environments. Learning through play, an age-old concept, has been shown to significantly enhance student understanding and retention of information. In this context, games and simulations can serve as powerful tools to illustrate complex concepts, foster collaboration, and stimulate critical thinking. Furthermore, with the advent of AI, educators now have the capability to tailor these interactive experiences more closely to their curriculum and the unique needs of their students.

AI prompt development for creating educational games and simulations involves understanding the core objectives of the lesson and translating these into interactive, game-based learning scenarios. By leveraging AI, educators can generate ideas and frameworks for games and simulations that not only align with educational standards but also captivate students' interests, thereby enhancing their learning experience.

Activity 1: Designing an AI-Generated Math Puzzle Game

Tools & Materials Needed:

- AI educational tool or platform

- Basic understanding of current math curriculum topics and objectives

- Access to a digital game creation tool or platform (optional)

Time Needed: 1-2 hours

Outcome: An engaging, AI-generated math puzzle game tailored to the current curriculum.

Instructions:

1. Define Game Objectives:

    ○ Identify key math concepts or skills from your curriculum that you wish to reinforce through the game.

2. Craft AI Prompts for Game Ideas:

    ○ Write specific AI prompts like "Generate ideas for a puzzle game that helps students practice [specific math concept] in a fun and engaging way."

3. Generate and Review Game Concepts:

    ○ Use the AI tool with your prompts to generate game ideas. Select the most suitable concept that aligns with your educational goals.

4. Develop the Game:

    ○ Depending on your resources, either use a digital game creation tool to bring the AI-generated concept to life or create a physical version of the game.

5. Implement and Observe:

    ○ Introduce the game to your students in a classroom setting. Observe their engagement, participation, and comprehension levels.

6. Post-Implementation AI Prompt for Educators:

  ○ "Analyze student feedback and performance data from the math puzzle game to identify areas for improvement and further customization."

Activity 2: Creating a Historical Simulation

Tools & Materials Needed:

- AI educational tool or content generator

- Information on a historical period or event from the curriculum

- Resources for creating simulations (digital tools, props, role-play scripts)

Time Needed: 2-3 hours

Outcome: An immersive, AI-generated historical simulation that enhances students' understanding of a specific period or event.

Instructions:

1. Select a Historical Topic:

   a. Choose a historical event or period that you are currently covering in your curriculum.

2. Formulate AI Prompts for Simulation Scenarios:

   a. Develop AI prompts such as "Create a detailed scenario for a simulation that immerses students in [historical period/event], highlighting the key figures, conflicts, and cultural aspects."

3. Generate and Adapt Scenarios:

   a. Input the prompts into the AI tool to generate simulation scenarios. Adapt these scenarios to suit your classroom resources and student needs.

4. Set Up and Conduct the Simulation:

   a. Prepare the classroom with necessary props or digital tools. Conduct the historical simulation, guiding students through the scenario and their assigned roles.

5. Debrief and Reflect:

   a. After the simulation, hold a debriefing session to discuss students' experiences, insights gained, and historical understandings.

Activity 3: Building an Environmental Science Ecosystem Simulation

Tools & Materials Needed:

- AI educational tool or simulation software

- List of key concepts and objectives for an environmental science unit

- Digital platform for creating or running simulations

Time Needed: 2-3 hours

Outcome: A dynamic, AI-generated simulation of an ecosystem, aiding students in understanding environmental science concepts.

Instructions:

1. Identify Key Concepts:

   - Determine which environmental science concepts you want to address through the simulation (e.g., food chains, pollution effects).

2. Generate AI Prompts for Simulation Content:

   - Create AI prompts like "Design a simulation scenario that demonstrates the impact of pollution on marine ecosystems and food chains."

3. Develop the Simulation:

   - Use the AI tool to generate content for the simulation. Utilize digital simulation software to create or adapt the AI-generated scenario.

4. Implement in Class:

   - Run the ecosystem simulation with your students. Allow them to interact with and alter the simulation to see different ecological outcomes.

5. Discuss and Analyze:

   - Facilitate a class discussion analyzing the simulation outcomes, linking back to the environmental science concepts covered.

By engaging in these activities, educators can leverage AI to create immersive, interactive learning experiences through games and simulations, providing students with a deeper understanding and a more engaging approach to curriculum topics. These AI-enhanced activities not only bolster comprehension but also cater to a variety of learning styles, making education a more inclusive and enjoyable journey.

3.4 Developing Collaborative Projects and Group Activities

Collaboration is a fundamental skill necessary for success in both academic and personal spheres. It fosters communication, problem-solving, and social interaction skills among students while promoting a sense of community and shared responsibility. In today's interconnected world, the ability to work effectively as part of a team is invaluable. Educators can play a crucial role in developing these skills by integrating collaborative projects and group activities into their curriculum.

Leveraging AI to design these collaborative experiences can add a layer of personalization and innovation, ensuring that the activities are not only educational but also engaging and relevant to students' interests and abilities. By constructing AI prompts that generate ideas for group projects or collaborative activities, educators can streamline the planning process and create more meaningful, impactful learning experiences.

Activity 1: AI-Generated Collaborative Research Project

Tools & Materials Needed:

- AI educational tool or platform

- Access to research materials and internet

- Criteria for successful collaboration and project guidelines

Time Needed: 2-3 class periods

Outcome: A completed group research project that aligns with curriculum objectives and enhances teamwork skills.

Instructions:

1. Define the Project Scope:

   ○ Determine a broad topic or question related to your curriculum that can be explored through collaborative research.

2. Craft AI Prompts for Project Ideas:

   ○ Develop AI prompts such as "Generate collaborative research project ideas related to [curriculum topic] that encourage diverse roles and contributions."

3. Generate and Assign Projects:

   ○ Input your AI prompts into the tool to create a list of project ideas. Assign each group a project that matches their interests and abilities.

4. Monitor and Support:

- Provide guidance and support as students work on their projects. Monitor the group dynamics and ensure that each member contributes.

5. Evaluate and Reflect:

- Assess the completed projects based on content, collaboration, and presentation. Facilitate a reflection session where groups discuss their teamwork and learning experiences.

6. Post-Implementation AI Prompt for Educators:

- "Analyze the effectiveness of collaborative dynamics and learning outcomes from the AI-generated research projects."

Activity 2: Designing a Collaborative Art Project

Tools & Materials Needed:

- AI educational tool or content generator

- Art supplies relevant to the project

- Criteria for successful collaboration and artistic expression

Time Needed: 2-3 class periods

Outcome: An artistic creation that reflects collaborative effort and creativity.

Instructions:

1. Identify Themes or Concepts:

- Choose themes or concepts from your curriculum that can be expressed through art.

2. Formulate AI Prompts for Art Projects:

- Write AI prompts like "Suggest ideas for a collaborative art project that illustrates [curriculum theme/concept] and allows for individual expression."

3. Generate and Plan the Art Project:

- Use the AI tool to generate project ideas. Plan the project, ensuring that it allows for individual contributions while contributing to a cohesive final piece.

4. Facilitate and Support:

○ Guide students as they collaborate on the art project. Encourage creativity, discussion, and mutual respect.

5. Present and Evaluate:

○ Have groups present their final artwork. Evaluate based on artistic expression, adherence to the theme, and collaborative effort.

Activity 3: Creating a Collaborative Science Experiment

Tools & Materials Needed:

- AI educational tool or platform

- Science lab materials or virtual lab software

- Guidelines for effective team-based experiments

Time Needed: 1-2 class periods

Outcome: A successfully executed science experiment that relies on teamwork and scientific inquiry.

Instructions:

1. Select an Experiment Topic:

○ Choose a topic or principle from your science curriculum suitable for a group experiment.

2. Develop AI Prompts for Experiment Ideas:

○ Create AI prompts such as "Generate ideas for a collaborative science experiment on [topic] that requires different roles for each team member."

3. Generate and Organize the Experiment:

○ Input the prompts into the AI tool and select an experiment idea. Assign roles and responsibilities to each group member based on the experiment's needs.

4. Conduct and Monitor:

○ Supervise as students conduct the experiment. Ensure that each member participates and contributes to their role.

5. Analyze and Discuss:

○ After completing the experiment, have each group analyze their results and discuss the collaborative process and scientific findings.

By implementing these activities, educators can effectively use AI to enhance the planning and execution of collaborative projects, providing students with valuable opportunities to develop their teamwork and problem-solving skills while deepening their understanding of academic content.

3.5 Leveraging AI for Real-Time Feedback and Adaptations

In modern educational environments, the ability to provide and utilize real-time feedback is transforming teaching and learning processes. Real-time feedback allows educators to make immediate adjustments to their teaching strategies, catering more effectively to the needs of their students and enhancing the overall learning experience. Leveraging AI for this purpose can significantly streamline the process, offering instant insights into student comprehension and engagement. This enables a more dynamic, responsive educational approach where teaching methods and materials can be adapted on the fly to address students' needs.

Interactive AI prompts play a crucial role in this context. They can be designed to generate instant feedback mechanisms, such as interactive quizzes, polls, and response systems, that actively involve students in their learning process. By integrating these AI-driven tools into classroom activities, educators can gain immediate understanding of student progress and areas of difficulty, facilitating timely and informed interventions.

Activity 1: AI-Enhanced Interactive Quizzes

Tools & Materials Needed:

- AI educational tool or platform capable of creating quizzes

- Access to a device and internet for each student

- Content for the quiz based on current lessons

Time Needed: 30 minutes

Outcome: An interactive, AI-generated quiz that provides real-time feedback on student understanding and engagement.

Instructions:

1. Prepare Content and AI Prompts:

   ○ Review the current lesson content and identify key concepts and objectives. Craft AI prompts like "Create a set of interactive quiz questions based on [lesson topic] that assesses understanding and prompts critical thinking."

2. Generate and Implement the Quiz:

- Input your AI prompts into the educational tool to generate a quiz. Implement this quiz in your classroom, using devices so each student can participate.

3. Analyze Real-Time Results:

- Review the instant feedback from the quiz to identify areas where students are excelling or struggling.

4. Adjust Teaching Based on Feedback:

- Use the insights gained from the quiz results to address misconceptions, reinforce concepts, or extend on topics where students show strong interest and understanding.

5. Post-Implementation AI Prompt for Educators:

- "Evaluate the effectiveness of the AI-generated quiz in identifying student comprehension issues and facilitating engagement."

Activity 2: Real-Time Feedback Polls

Tools & Materials Needed:

- AI tool for generating educational polls

- Classroom response system or devices capable of submitting poll responses

- Current unit or lesson plan topics

Time Needed: 20 minutes

Outcome: Insightful student feedback on a specific topic, facilitating immediate classroom adjustments.

Instructions:

1. Identify Discussion Points:

- Choose topics or concepts from your current lesson where student feedback would be valuable.

2. Craft AI Prompts for Poll Questions:

- Develop AI prompts like "Generate poll questions that gauge students' opinions and understanding of [specific concept or topic]."

3. Conduct and Monitor the Poll:

○ Use the AI-generated questions to create a poll. Conduct this poll in class, allowing students to respond via the response system or devices.

4. Analyze and Respond:

○ Review poll results in real-time. Use this feedback to facilitate a class discussion, clarify misconceptions, or delve deeper into topics of interest.

Activity 3: AI-Driven Instant Response System for Open-Ended Questions

Tools & Materials Needed:

- AI interactive tool capable of analyzing open-ended responses

- Devices for students to submit their responses

- Topics or questions related to current learning material

Time Needed: 30-40 minutes

Outcome: A better understanding of student thoughts and detailed feedback on specific subjects, guiding immediate classroom dynamics.

Instructions:

1. Prepare Open-Ended Questions:

○ Identify areas within the current curriculum where student input would provide valuable insights. Formulate AI prompts like "Generate open-ended questions that encourage students to express their thoughts on [subject or concept]."

2. Set Up Instant Response System:

○ Input the AI-generated questions into the response system. Explain the activity to students and ensure they understand how to submit their answers.

3. Collect and Analyze Responses:

○ As responses come in, use the AI tool to analyze them for common themes, misconceptions, or unique insights.

4. Facilitate Discussion and Adapt Lessons:

○ Based on the analysis, lead a class discussion addressing the main points raised by students. Adapt your lesson plan or teaching approach based on this feedback to better meet student needs.

By implementing these activities, educators can effectively utilize AI to facilitate real-time feedback in their classrooms, allowing for immediate adjustments and fostering a more responsive and engaging learning environment. This not only enhances student comprehension but also promotes a sense of participation and belonging in the classroom.

Chapter Four

Prompts for Enhancing Creativity and Critical Thinking

4.1 Crafting Prompts for Creative Writing and Artistic Projects

Creative expression is an essential component of comprehensive education, offering students the opportunity to explore their identities, experiences, and perspectives in unique and personal ways. Engaging in creative writing and artistic projects not only enhances students' ability to express themselves but also bolsters their critical thinking, innovation, and emotional intelligence. In this digital era, AI can serve as a remarkable tool to generate diverse and inspiring prompts that encourage students to push the boundaries of their creativity and engage more deeply with their learning material.

Crafting AI prompts for creative projects involves understanding the elements that spark creativity within your students. These prompts should challenge them, yet provide enough scope for personal interpretation and expression. Educators can leverage AI to produce a wide array of imaginative and thought-provoking prompts tailored to the interests and abilities of their students, thereby enriching the educational experience and fostering a more engaging learning environment.

Activity 1: AI-Generated Prompts for Creative Writing

Tools & Materials Needed:

- AI educational tool or platform capable of generating writing prompts

- Writing materials (computers, notebooks, etc.)

- Criteria for assessing creative writing (originality, coherence, use of language)

Time Needed: 1 hour

Outcome: Original student compositions inspired by AI-generated creative writing prompts.

Instructions:

1. Determine Writing Focus:

    ○ Decide on a theme, genre, or topic for the creative writing assignment that aligns with your curriculum or students' interests.

2. Craft AI Prompts for Writing:

    ○ Write specific AI prompts such as "Generate a creative writing prompt that involves a mystery set in a historical period we've studied" or "Create a writing prompt that encourages students to imagine the future of technology."

3. Generate and Distribute Prompts:

    ○ Use the AI tool with your prompts to create a variety of creative writing prompts. Distribute different prompts to students or let them choose their favorite.

4. Facilitate Writing and Reflection:

    ○ Allow students time to write their pieces. Encourage them to reflect on their writing process and how the prompt influenced their creativity.

5. Share and Assess:

    ○ Organize a session where students share their work with the class. Assess the compositions based on predefined criteria, focusing on creativity and engagement with the prompt.

Activity 2: Designing AI-Inspired Art Projects

Tools & Materials Needed:

- AI tool for generating artistic project ideas

- Art supplies corresponding to the project (paint, clay, digital art software, etc.)

- Evaluation criteria for artistic projects (creativity, technique, interpretation)

Time Needed: 2-3 hours

Outcome: Unique art projects conceptualized from AI-generated prompts, reflecting students' interpretation and creativity.

Instructions:

1. Identify Artistic Goals:

   ○ Choose a goal or theme for the art project, considering current curriculum topics or student interests.

2. Develop AI Prompts for Art Projects:

   ○ Formulate AI prompts like "Generate ideas for an art project that explores the concept of freedom" or "Provide a prompt for creating a piece of art that represents a significant moment in history."

3. Produce and Implement Art Ideas:

   ○ Input your AI prompts into the tool to generate artistic project ideas. Present these ideas to the students and let them select which they'd like to pursue.

4. Create and Reflect:

   ○ Provide students with the necessary materials and time to create their art projects. Encourage them to reflect on how the prompt influenced their artistic choices and expression.

5. Exhibit and Evaluate:

   ○ Display the completed art projects in class or a school exhibition. Evaluate the projects based on your criteria, highlighting creativity and connection to the prompt.

Activity 3: AI-Prompted Collaborative Storytelling

Tools & Materials Needed:

- AI tool capable of generating storytelling prompts

- Digital document platform or physical writing materials for group collaboration

- Guidelines for collaborative storytelling (roles, length, themes)

Time Needed: 1-2 hours

Outcome: Collaboratively written stories that combine the creative insights and styles of multiple students, sparked by AI-generated prompts.

Instructions:

1. Set Objectives for Storytelling:

   ○ Determine the objectives and constraints for the collaborative story-telling project, such as theme, length, or specific elements that must be included.

2. Generate AI Storytelling Prompts:

   ○ Create AI prompts like "Generate a storytelling starter that incorporates elements of fantasy and requires a moral resolution" or "Create a scenario that prompts a story about overcoming challenges."

3. Initiate Collaborative Writing:

   ○ Divide students into small groups and assign each group an AI-generated prompt. Explain the rules and objectives of collaborative storytelling.

4. Write and Collaborate:

   ○ Have groups work together to develop stories based on their prompts.

   ○ Encourage creativity, cooperation, and respect for each member's ideas.

5. Share and Discuss:

   ○ Allow each group to share their story with the class. Discuss the different approaches, ideas, and how the AI prompts influenced their narratives.

By integrating these activities, educators can effectively use AI to enhance creativity and collaboration within the classroom, providing students with unique opportunities to express themselves and engage with content in meaningful, innovative ways.

4.2 Developing Critical Thinking through AI Scenarios

Critical thinking is a cornerstone of education, equipping students with the ability to analyze complex concepts, identify underlying problems, and develop effective solutions. It transcends traditional memorization and regurgitation of information, encouraging students to delve deeper into subjects and consider various perspectives. AI can significantly aid in this developmental process by generating scenarios, case studies, and ethical dilemmas tailored to specific learning objectives. These AI-generated situations provide real-world context that challenges students to employ their analytical skills and make informed decisions.

By crafting AI prompts aimed at developing critical thinking, educators can produce a variety of thought-provoking scenarios that resonate with their curriculum and students' everyday lives. This approach not only enhances students' problem-solving abilities but also prepares them for real-world challenges by fostering adaptability, creativity, and resilience.

Activity 1: Analyzing AI-Generated Ethical Dilemmas

Tools & Materials Needed:

- AI educational tool or platform
- Criteria for evaluating ethical arguments and decision-making
- Digital or physical platform for presenting scenarios and recording responses

Time Needed: 1 hour

Outcome: Enhanced student ability to analyze, discuss, and resolve ethical dilemmas.

Instructions:

1. Identify Learning Goals:

   ○ Determine the ethical concepts or dilemmas relevant to your curriculum or current societal issues.

2. Craft AI Prompts for Ethical Dilemmas:

   ○ Write specific AI prompts such as "Generate an ethical dilemma related to [topic] that requires critical analysis and decision-making from a [specific perspective or role]."

3. Generate and Present Dilemmas:

   ○ Use the AI tool with your prompts to create ethical dilemmas. Present these dilemmas to the class and assign them roles or perspectives for the discussion.

4. Facilitate Class Discussion or Debate:

   ○ Organize a structured discussion or debate on the dilemmas, guiding students to consider different angles and consequences of potential decisions.

5. Evaluate and Reflect:

   ○ Assess students' engagement, reasoning, and decision-making during the discussion. Lead a reflection session to highlight learning points and areas for improvement.

Activity 2: Solving AI-Generated Case Studies

Tools & Materials Needed:

- AI educational tool capable of generating case studies

- Criteria for analyzing case study solutions

- Platform for students to present their findings (presentation software, posters, etc.)

Time Needed: 2 hours

Outcome: Improved student proficiency in analyzing, solving, and presenting solutions to real-world problems.

Instructions:

1. Select Relevant Topics:

   ○ Choose real-world issues or topics from your subject area that are suitable for case study analysis.

2. Develop AI Prompts for Case Studies:

   ○ Formulate AI prompts like "Create a detailed case study on [subject/topic] that presents a complex problem needing resolution."

3. Create and Assign Case Studies:

   ○ Generate case studies using the AI tool and assign them to student groups, ensuring each group has a different scenario.

4. Analyze and Solve:

   ○ Have student groups analyze their assigned case studies, develop solutions, and prepare presentations outlining their reasoning and conclusions.

5. Present and Discuss:

   ○ Allow each group to present their case study and proposed solutions. Facilitate a class-wide discussion comparing the approaches and outcomes.

Activity 3: Interactive Scenario-Based Problem Solving

Tools & Materials Needed:

- AI tool for generating scenarios

- Classroom technology for interactive engagement (smartboard, computers, tablets)

- Rubric for assessing problem-solving and critical thinking skills

Time Needed: 1-2 hours

Outcome: Enhanced student engagement and critical thinking through interactive scenario-based activities.

Instructions:

1. Define Problem-Solving Scenarios:

   ○ Identify key themes or challenges relevant to your curriculum that can be transformed into problem-solving scenarios.

2. Generate AI Prompts for Scenarios:

   ○ Create AI prompts such as "Design an interactive scenario involving [curriculum theme] that requires students to employ critical thinking and problem-solving skills."

3. Implement Interactive Scenarios:

   ○ Use the AI-generated scenarios in class, leveraging technology to make the experience interactive. This could involve group discussions, digital simulations, or decision-making trees.

4. Guide and Monitor:

   ○ Guide students through the scenarios, providing hints or questions that spur deeper thinking and discussion. Monitor their decision-making processes and how they approach problems.

5. Debrief and Reflect:

   ○ After completing the scenarios, debrief with the class. Discuss the different approaches, solutions, and the rationale behind their decisions.

6. Post-Implementation AI Prompt for Educators:

   ○ "Generate a follow-up questionnaire to assess students' perception of their critical thinking and problem-solving skills after participating in AI-generated scenarios."

By engaging in these activities, educators can provide students with valuable opportunities to apply critical thinking and analytical skills in diverse contexts, fostering a deeper understanding and practical application of their knowledge.

4.3 Integrating Problem-Solving Activities

Problem-solving activities are pivotal in the educational landscape, serving not just as a means to apply learned concepts, but also as avenues for students to develop critical analytical skills and resilience. Engaging students with real-world problems encourages them to think critically, work collaboratively, and persevere through challenges, thereby preparing them for future personal and professional endeavors. Integrating AI into this process can provide a dynamic and relevant dimension to problem-solving activities, making them more aligned with current global issues and technological advancements.

AI prompt development for problem-solving activities involves identifying real-world issues or theoretical problems that correspond with the curriculum and student interests. By crafting AI prompts that generate complex, curriculum-aligned problems, educators can offer students a variety of scenarios that challenge their understanding and provoke innovative thinking and solutions.

Activity 1: AI-Generated Environmental Challenges

Tools & Materials Needed:

- AI educational tool capable of generating real-world problems

- Access to research resources (books, internet, scientific reports)

- Project presentation tools (software for slides, posters, or videos)

Time Needed: 3-4 class periods

Outcome: Detailed student projects addressing AI-generated environmental challenges with researched solutions and action plans.

Instructions:

1. Identify Environmental Themes:

   ○ Choose broad environmental themes relevant to your curriculum, such as climate change, biodiversity, or sustainable living.

2. Develop AI Prompts for Environmental Challenges:

   ○ Write AI prompts such as "Generate a real-world problem related to [chosen environmental theme] that requires a sustainable solution."

3. Generate and Assign Challenges:

   ○ Use the AI tool with your prompts to create a list of environmental challenges. Assign different challenges to student groups.

4. Research and Develop Solutions:

   ○ Students research their assigned problems, focusing on underlying causes, global impacts, and existing solutions. They then develop their innovative solutions or action plans.

5. Present and Evaluate:

   ○ Each group presents their research findings and proposed solutions. Evaluate based on criteria like feasibility, creativity, and scientific accuracy.

6. Post-Implementation AI Prompt for Educators:

   ○ "Generate a reflection questionnaire for students to evaluate their problem-solving process and learning outcomes from the environmental challenge activity."

Activity 2: AI-Generated Math Puzzles for Logical Thinking

Tools & Materials Needed:

- AI educational tool for generating math problems

- Classroom set of computers or tablets

- Criteria for assessing logical reasoning and problem-solving skills

Time Needed: 1-2 class periods

Outcome: Improved student logical thinking and problem-solving skills through AI-generated math puzzles.

Instructions:

1. Select Math Concepts:

   ○ Identify key math concepts or units that students are currently studying or find challenging.

2. Craft AI Prompts for Math Puzzles:

   ○ Develop AI prompts like "Create complex math puzzles that require logical thinking to solve, based on [specific math concept or unit]."

3. Generate and Distribute Puzzles:

   ○ Input your AI prompts into the educational tool to generate math puzzles. Distribute these puzzles to students, either individually or in small groups.

4. Solve and Discuss:

- ○ Allow time for students to work on the puzzles, encouraging collaboration and discussion. Assist and guide as needed.

5. Review and Reflect:

- ○ Review the solutions as a class, discussing different approaches and strategies. Reflect on the problem-solving process and areas of difficulty.

Activity 3: Collaborative AI-Generated Business Simulations

Tools & Materials Needed:

- AI tool for generating business scenarios or simulations

- Access to business planning resources or simulation platforms

- Criteria for assessing teamwork, business strategy, and problem-solving

Time Needed: 2-3 class periods

Outcome: Engaging and insightful business simulation projects that challenge students to develop and apply business strategies in a collaborative setting.

Instructions:

1. Identify Business Principles:

- ○ Determine the business principles or concepts you wish to reinforce, considering current lessons or student interest areas.

2. Develop AI Prompts for Business Simulations:

- ○ Formulate AI prompts such as "Design a business simulation scenario that challenges students to address [specific business issue or principle], considering market conditions and competition."

3. Create and Implement Simulations:

- ○ Use the AI tool to generate business simulation scenarios. Divide students into 'company' teams and assign each a scenario.

4. Develop Business Strategies:

- ○ Teams work together to analyze their scenario, develop a business strategy, and plan how to overcome challenges presented in the simulation.

5. Present and Review:

- ○ Teams present their business strategies and outcomes. Review each presentation, focusing on creativity, feasibility, and application of business principles.

By engaging in these activities, educators can effectively use AI to enhance problem-solving exercises, providing students with valuable opportunities to apply their knowledge and skills in realistic, complex scenarios. This not only improves their analytical and decision-making abilities but also prepares them for real-life challenges.

4.4 Encouraging Exploration and Inquiry

Fostering curiosity and promoting an inquiry-based learning environment are essential for cultivating students' love of learning and their ability to think critically and innovatively. When students are encouraged to ask questions, explore, and seek out answers, they become more engaged, take ownership of their learning, and develop a deeper understanding of the subject matter. Interactive AI prompts can play a significant role in this process by generating thought-provoking questions and scenarios that push students to explore beyond the surface level of topics and engage with material in a more meaningful way.

Educators can utilize AI to craft prompts that not only align with the curriculum but also open doors to new ideas, perspectives, and interdisciplinary connections. By implementing inquiry-based activities driven by AI, teachers can create a dynamic learning environment where students feel empowered to investigate and discover.

Activity 1: AI-Generated Inquiry Projects

Tools & Materials Needed:

- AI educational tool or platform capable of generating inquiry-based questions

- Access to research materials and internet

- Presentation tools (software, boards, etc.)

Time Needed: 2-3 class periods

Outcome: Completed student inquiry projects based on AI-generated questions, fostering deeper understanding and curiosity.

Instructions:

1. Select a Broad Topic:

   ○ Choose a broad topic relevant to your curriculum that can spark diverse inquiries, such as "ecosystems," "civil rights movements," or "space exploration."

2. Develop AI Prompts for Inquiry Questions:

     ○ Create specific AI prompts like "Generate open-ended questions about [chosen topic] that encourage deep exploration and research."

3. Generate and Assign Inquiry Questions:

     ○ Use the AI tool with your prompts to produce a range of inquiry questions. Assign different questions to student groups or let them choose based on interest.

4. Guide the Inquiry Process:

     ○ Provide students with resources and guidance to research their questions. Encourage them to use various sources and to document their findings and thought processes.

5. Present and Reflect:

     ○ Have students present their research and findings. Facilitate a class discussion reflecting on the inquiry process, what was learned, and how questions led to further questions and discoveries.

Activity 2: AI-Inspired Science Exploration Day

Tools & Materials Needed:

- AI tool for generating science exploration prompts

- Science lab materials or access to virtual lab simulations

- Observation and recording tools (notebooks, tablets)

Time Needed: 1 class period

Outcome: Engaged and curious students actively participating in hands-on science explorations.

Instructions:

1. Identify Key Science Concepts:

     ○ Select key concepts from your science curriculum that lend themselves to hands-on exploration, like chemical reactions, plant biology, or physics principles.

2. Formulate AI Prompts for Exploration Activities:

     ○ Write AI prompts such as "Create hands-on science activities that allow students to explore [science concept] through experimentation."

3. Generate and Organize Exploration Stations:

○ Use the AI-generated activities to set up exploration stations around the classroom or lab. Ensure each station has clear instructions and necessary materials.

4. Facilitate and Monitor Explorations:

○ Allow students to rotate through stations, conducting experiments and making observations. Guide them to ask questions and make predictions based on their explorations.

5. Debrief and Extend Learning:

○ Gather students to discuss their observations and findings. Encourage them to ask further questions and suggest how they might explore these concepts beyond the classroom.

Activity 3: Historical Inquiry and Debate Session

Tools & Materials Needed:

- AI educational tool for generating historical scenarios or dilemmas

- Resources for historical research (books, articles, online databases)

- Tools for debate (timer, microphone, debate guidelines)

Time Needed: 2-3 class periods

Outcome: A deeper understanding of historical events and issues through research-driven debates based on AI-generated scenarios.

Instructions:

1. Choose a Historical Period or Issue:

○ Pick a period or issue from history that offers multiple perspectives and is relevant to your curriculum.

2. Generate AI Prompts for Historical Scenarios:

○ Develop AI prompts like "Generate complex historical scenarios or dilemmas from [chosen period/issue] that can be explored from multiple viewpoints."

3. Create and Assign Research Topics:

○ Use the AI tool to generate scenarios and assign them to groups of students. Each group should research their scenario, focusing on different perspectives.

4. Prepare and Conduct Debates:

- Have each group present their findings in a structured debate format, defending their perspective based on their research.

5. Reflect and Evaluate:

- After the debates, lead a class reflection on the different perspectives presented and the importance of evidence-based arguments. Discuss how the activity changed or deepened their understanding of the historical issue.

By implementing these activities, educators not only stimulate curiosity and inquiry among students but also harness the power of AI to create a more engaging and thought-provoking learning environment. This approach encourages students to become active participants in their education, fostering a lifelong love of learning and discovery.

4.5 Applying Creativity and Critical Thinking to Real-World Contexts

In today's rapidly changing world, equipping students with the ability to apply creative and critical thinking skills to real-world contexts is more important than ever. These skills empower students to tackle complex social, environmental, and technological challenges, fostering a sense of agency and responsibility. By integrating solution-based AI prompts into the curriculum, educators can guide students in conceptualizing and developing innovative solutions to pressing issues, thus bridging the gap between academic learning and practical application.

Solution-based AI prompts encourage students to think beyond conventional boundaries and envisage creative solutions to real-life problems. They stimulate inquiry, provoke discussion, and encourage a multidisciplinary approach to problem-solving. Through structured activities, students can learn to harness their creativity and critical thinking to make tangible contributions to their community and the world at large.

Activity 1: Tackling Environmental Challenges

Tools & Materials Needed:

- AI educational tool for generating problem scenarios

- Access to research tools and internet

- Materials for creating presentations (e.g., poster boards, digital presentation software)

Time Needed: 3-4 class periods

Outcome: Student-developed solutions to real-world environmental challenges, presented in a compelling format.

Instructions:

1. Set the Scene:

   ○ Begin by discussing current environmental issues and the importance of sustainable solutions. Highlight the role of innovation and critical thinking in addressing these challenges.

2. Generate AI Prompts for Environmental Challenges:

   ○ Use AI prompts such as "Generate current real-world environmental challenges that require innovative solutions" and "Provide background information on these challenges."

3. Research and Brainstorm:

   ○ Divide students into groups and assign each group a challenge generated by the AI. Each group researches their assigned issue, considering causes, impacts, and existing solutions.

4. Develop Solutions:

   ○ Students brainstorm and develop innovative solutions to their assigned environmental challenges. Encourage them to think creatively and consider sustainability, feasibility, and impact.

5. Create and Present Solutions:

   ○ Groups create presentations outlining their research findings and proposed solutions. Ensure presentations cover the rationale, expected outcomes, and implementation steps of the solution.

6. Feedback Session:

   ○ After presentations, conduct a feedback session where students critique and discuss each other's solutions, focusing on creativity, practicality, and potential impact.

Activity 2: Designing Solutions for Community Issues

Tools & Materials Needed:

- AI tool for generating community problems

- Materials for project development (charts, models, digital tools)

- Guidelines for evaluating solutions

Time Needed: 2-3 class periods

Outcome: Practical solutions to community-specific problems, developed using critical thinking and creativity.

Instructions:

1. Identify Community Needs:

   ○ Engage students in a discussion about local community needs and issues that they observe or experience.

2. Generate AI Prompts for Community Problems:

   ○ Develop AI prompts like "List significant, solvable community issues in [local area]" and "Describe these issues in detail."

3. Assign Research and Solution Development:

   ○ Assign each student or group a community issue identified by the AI. They research the problem, its scope, and existing attempts at solutions.

4. Solution Proposal and Development:

   ○ Students devise creative solutions to their assigned problems. They should consider the feasibility, cost, and potential barriers to their solutions.

5. Prototype and Presentation:

   ○ If possible, students create a prototype or detailed plan for their solutions. They then present their ideas to the class, explaining how their solutions address the specific needs of the community.

Activity 3: Innovating for Future Technologies

Tools & Materials Needed:

- AI educational platform for scenario generation

- Access to current technological trends and research materials

- Digital tools for designing prototypes or conceptual models

Time Needed: 3-4 class periods

Outcome: Innovative concepts for future technologies that address current technological challenges or needs.

Instructions:

1. Explore Technological Trends:

- Start with a discussion on recent technological advances and their impacts on society. Discuss the concept of innovation and its importance.

2. Craft AI Prompts for Technological Challenges:

- Use AI prompts like "Identify emerging technological challenges that could have significant social impacts" and "Suggest areas in technology that require innovation for future development."

3. Research and Ideation:

- Students research the technological challenges generated by the AI. They brainstorm ideas for new technologies or innovations that could address these challenges.

4. Develop and Design:

- Students select their best ideas and develop them further, considering practicality, impact, and implementation. They create conceptual designs or models for their proposed technologies.

5. Present and Critique:

- Students present their technology concepts to the class, outlining the problem, their proposed solution, and the potential impact. Engage the class in critiquing and discussing the feasibility and potential of each concept.

These activities not only enhance students' problem-solving and critical thinking skills but also encourage them to apply what they have learned to real-world scenarios, fostering a deeper understanding and a greater sense of responsibility toward societal and environmental issues.

Chapter Five

Prompts for Assessment and Feedback

5.1 Automating Grading with AI

The integration of AI into the grading process offers the potential to streamline assessment, reduce the time educators spend on grading, and provide students with immediate feedback. Utilizing AI for grading can enhance the consistency and objectivity of assessments, especially for quantitative assignments and standardized tests. However, educators need to navigate challenges such as ensuring the AI's grading criteria align closely with the learning objectives and maintaining transparency in the assessment process.

By crafting AI prompts for grading, educators can tailor AI systems to accurately assess student submissions based on predefined criteria or rubrics. This customization is crucial for ensuring that AI-assisted grading aligns with educational standards and accurately reflects student understanding and performance.

Activity 1: Setting Up AI for Multiple-Choice Quizzes

Tools & Materials Needed:

- AI grading tool compatible with multiple-choice formats

- Set of multiple-choice questions (MCQs) and answer keys

- Sample student responses (real or fabricated for testing purposes)

Time Needed: 1-2 hours

Outcome: A functional AI-assisted grading system for multiple-choice quizzes, set up and calibrated for accuracy and fairness.

Instructions:

1. Prepare the Quiz and Answer Key:

   ○ Compile a set of MCQs relevant to your curriculum. Create an answer key for these questions.

2. Develop AI Grading Prompts:

   ○ Write AI prompts like "Grade these multiple-choice responses based on the provided answer key, highlighting any common misconceptions indicated by incorrect answers."

3. Test the AI Grading System:

   ○ Enter your MCQs, answer key, and AI prompts into the grading tool. Use sample student responses to test the AI's grading accuracy.

4. Evaluate AI Grading Results:

   ○ Compare the AI's grading results with manual grading to assess accuracy. Note any discrepancies or patterns in misgrading.

5. Adjust and Refine:

   ○ Based on the evaluation, refine the AI prompts or grading parameters as needed to improve accuracy and alignment with learning objectives.

Activity 2: Automating Short-Answer Grading

Tools & Materials Needed:

- AI grading platform capable of evaluating short-answer responses

- List of short-answer questions and model answers

- Collection of anonymized student responses

Time Needed: 2-3 hours

Outcome: An AI-assisted grading system tailored for short-answer assessments, with evaluated effectiveness and fairness.

Instructions:

1. Compile Questions and Model Answers:

   ○ Select several short-answer questions from recent assignments. Develop comprehensive model answers for each.

2. Formulate AI Grading Prompts:

- Create specific AI prompts such as "Assess these short-answer submissions by comparing them to the model answers, and identify key areas where students commonly struggle."

3. Implement AI Grading:

- Input the short-answer questions, model answers, and AI prompts into the grading platform. Run a batch of anonymized student responses through the system.

4. Analyze Grading Discrepancies:

- Review the AI's grading outcomes against manual grading to identify any inaccuracies or biases, especially in understanding students' explanations.

5. Refine AI Parameters and Feedback:

- Adjust the AI grading criteria based on your analysis to enhance grading fairness and detailed feedback provision.

Activity 3: Developing AI-Assisted Rubric for Project Evaluations

Tools & Materials Needed:

- AI grading software with capabilities for rubric-based assessment

- Detailed project rubric with specific criteria and scales

- Examples of student projects for testing

Time Needed: 3-4 hours

Outcome: A reliable AI-powered system for grading student projects according to a detailed rubric, ensuring consistency and objective assessment.

Instructions:

1. Create a Detailed Grading Rubric:

- Develop a comprehensive rubric for the student project, outlining clear criteria, indicators of performance, and scoring scales.

2. Generate AI Grading Prompts:

- Construct AI prompts like "Evaluate student projects against the provided rubric, assigning scores for each criterion and offering constructive feedback."

3. Test and Calibrate the AI System:

- Enter the grading rubric and AI prompts into the grading software. Use a set of varied student projects to test the AI's evaluation capabilities.

4. Compare and Contrast Grading Outcomes:

- Analyze differences between AI-generated grades and manual assessments. Identify any inconsistencies or areas where the AI may misinterpret the rubric.

5. Adjust AI Settings and Rubric Definitions:

- Refine the AI's settings and clarify rubric criteria based on the comparative analysis to ensure that the AI grading aligns closely with educator expectations and standards.

6. Post-Implementation AI Prompt for Educators:

- "Analyze the distribution of AI-generated grades for patterns or biases and collect student feedback on the perceived fairness and clarity of AI-assisted feedback."

Through these activities, educators can thoughtfully integrate AI into the grading process, enhancing efficiency while ensuring that the technology supports educational objectives and fair assessment practices.

5.2 Generating Constructive Feedback

Providing detailed and constructive feedback is vital to student growth and understanding. Effective feedback not only guides students in their current assignments but also aids in developing their skills for future tasks. In the context of education, feedback should serve as a mirror, reflecting students' performance in a way that highlights their strengths and pinpoints areas for improvement. Integrating AI into the feedback process can streamline and enhance this practice, offering personalized, consistent, and timely responses to student work.

AI can be programmed to recognize key elements in student submissions, comparing them against established criteria and generating feedback that is both informative and encouraging. By crafting specific AI prompts, educators can ensure that the feedback generated aligns with learning objectives and addresses individual student needs.

Activity 1: AI-Generated Feedback on Writing Assignments

Tools & Materials Needed:

- AI educational tool capable of analyzing text and generating feedback

- Collection of student writing assignments

- Rubric or criteria for evaluating writing assignments

Time Needed: 2-3 hours

Outcome: Personalized, AI-generated feedback for student writing assignments that aligns with educational goals and standards.

Instructions:

1. Prepare Writing Assignments and Criteria:

   ○ Collect a set of student writing assignments. Develop or revise your rubric detailing the criteria for assessment such as clarity, argumentation, grammar, and creativity.

2. Craft AI Prompts for Feedback Generation:

   ○ Write AI prompts like "Generate personalized feedback for a [specific type of writing] assignment focusing on [list criteria], highlighting strengths and areas for improvement."

3. Input Assignments and Generate Feedback:

   ○ Enter the writing assignments and AI prompts into the educational tool. Review the AI-generated feedback to ensure it meets your standards and aligns with the rubric.

4. Compare AI and Educator Feedback:

   ○ Compare the feedback generated by the AI with your own feedback on several assignments. Note differences in focus, tone, and completeness.

5. Adjust AI Settings or Prompts Based on Comparison:

   ○ Refine the AI prompts or settings based on your comparison to better align the AI-generated feedback with your educational objectives and feedback style.

Activity 2: Enhancing Math Problem-Solving Feedback

Tools & Materials Needed:

- AI tool with capabilities for analyzing mathematical reasoning

- Set of completed student math assignments or problem sets

- Guidelines or rubric for math problem-solving

Time Needed: 1-2 hours

Outcome: Constructive, AI-generated feedback on student math assignments that supports learning and improvement.

Instructions:

1. Collect Math Assignments and Define Evaluation Criteria:

    ○ Gather a collection of student solutions to math problems. Define clear criteria for evaluation, including computational accuracy, problem-solving strategies, and reasoning.

2. Develop AI Prompts for Feedback:

    ○ Construct AI prompts such as "Provide detailed feedback on these math problem solutions, assessing computational accuracy, conceptual understanding, and problem-solving approach."

3. Process Assignments Through AI:

    ○ Input the completed assignments and AI prompts into the tool. Allow the AI to analyze the solutions and generate feedback based on your criteria.

4. Review and Analyze AI Feedback:

    ○ Examine the AI-generated feedback for each assignment. Assess its relevance, helpfulness, and alignment with your evaluation criteria.

5. Refine Feedback and Discuss with Students:

    ○ Make any necessary adjustments to the feedback before sharing it with students. Discuss the AI feedback in class, encouraging reflection and understanding.

Activity 3: AI-Assisted Feedback for Project-Based Learning

Tools & Materials Needed:

- AI feedback tool capable of evaluating project-based work

- Collection of student projects

- Project evaluation rubric with detailed criteria

Time Needed: 2-3 hours

Outcome: Detailed, personalized feedback on student projects, aiding in reflection and future project improvement.

Instructions:

1. Prepare Student Projects and Rubric:

   ○ Assemble student projects for review. Ensure you have a detailed rubric that includes criteria such as research depth, creativity, application, and presentation.

2. Generate AI Feedback Prompts:

   ○ Create AI prompts tailored to project assessment, such as "Analyze this student project according to the provided rubric. Generate comprehensive feedback that identifies strengths and suggests areas for improvement based on each criterion."

3. Implement AI Analysis and Feedback Generation:

   ○ Enter the student projects and AI prompts into the feedback tool. Allow the AI to assess each project and produce feedback.

4. Evaluate and Refine AI-Generated Feedback:

   ○ Review the feedback provided by the AI for accuracy, relevance, and constructiveness. Adjust the AI prompts or settings if necessary to ensure feedback meets your standards.

5. Share Feedback and Facilitate Reflection:

   ○ Provide students with the AI-generated feedback along with your own observations if necessary. Facilitate a class discussion or individual reflection sessions to help students interpret and use the feedback for growth.

6. Post-Implementation AI Prompt for Educators:

   ○ "Generate a reflective questionnaire for students to assess the helpfulness and clarity of AI-generated feedback in enhancing their project-based learning experience."

Through these activities, educators can harness AI's potential to provide timely and constructive feedback, enabling students to reflect on their work, recognize their strengths, and identify areas for improvement in real time. This approach not only streamlines the feedback process but also enhances the overall learning experience by fostering a continuous cycle of improvement and deeper understanding.

5.3 Identifying Learning Patterns and Gaps

Utilizing AI to scrutinize student data presents an unparalleled opportunity to uncover and understand learning patterns, misconceptions, and gaps. This data-driven approach enables educators to tailor their teaching strategies more effectively, ensuring that each student receives the support they need to overcome challenges and enhance their understanding. By analyzing trends in student performance, educators can pinpoint common areas of difficulty and address them promptly, leading to improved educational outcomes.

Interactive AI prompts specifically designed for educational analysis can assist educators in extracting actionable insights from a wide range of student data. This process involves not only the identification of areas where students frequently struggle but also the recognition of successful strategies and topics where students excel. Armed with this knowledge, educators can make informed decisions to foster a more supportive and effective learning environment.

Activity 1: Analyzing Test Results for Common Misconceptions

Tools & Materials Needed:

- AI analysis tool capable of processing test results

- A set of recent student test results (anonymized)

- Access to the related test or assessment materials

Time Needed: 1-2 hours

Outcome: Identified common misconceptions or learning gaps based on AI analysis of test results.

Instructions:

1. Prepare the Test Data:

    ○ Collect the recent test results from your class. Ensure the data is anonymized and formatted correctly for analysis.

2. Develop AI Analysis Prompts:

    ○ Write AI prompts such as "Identify common errors and misconceptions in this set of student test results for [specific subject or topic]."

3. Conduct the AI Analysis:

    ○ Input the test results and AI prompts into the analysis tool. Allow the AI to process the data and identify patterns of common errors or misconceptions.

4. Review AI Insights:

    ○ Examine the AI-generated report on student misconceptions and learning gaps. Note any trends or recurring issues.

5. Plan Targeted Interventions:

- Based on the AI findings, plan targeted instructional interventions or review sessions that address the identified misconceptions and gaps.

Activity 2: AI-Driven Homework Pattern Analysis

Tools & Materials Needed:

- AI tool with the capability to analyze homework submissions

- A collection of recent student homework assignments

- Criteria or key concepts that the homework aimed to assess

Time Needed: 1-2 hours

Outcome: Insights into learning patterns and areas where students need additional support, informed by AI analysis.

Instructions:

1. Aggregate Homework Data:

- Gather recent homework assignments from students. Ensure they relate to key learning objectives or concepts.

2. Craft AI Prompts for Pattern Analysis:

- Create AI prompts like "Analyze patterns in student responses to homework on [topic], identifying frequent errors and areas of strong performance."

3. Perform AI Analysis:

- Input the homework data and AI prompts into the tool. Allow the AI to identify trends in student understanding and performance.

4. Interpret and Act on Insights:

- Review the AI-generated insights. Look for patterns that indicate where students excel and where they struggle.

5. Implement Supportive Measures:

- Develop lesson plans, resources, or supplemental activities that address the specific areas of difficulty highlighted by the AI analysis.

Activity 3: Project Feedback Compilation and Analysis

Tools & Materials Needed:

- AI analysis software suitable for evaluating textual feedback

- Collection of feedback given on recent student projects

- List of learning objectives or skills the projects were designed to assess

Time Needed: 2-3 hours

Outcome: A comprehensive understanding of student performance trends and individual learning gaps based on AI analysis of project feedback.

Instructions:

1. Compile Project Feedback:

   - Collect all the feedback provided on a set of student projects. Organize the feedback by project or learning objective.

2. Generate AI Analysis Prompts:

   - Formulate AI prompts such as "Summarize the key points of feedback on student projects regarding [specific learning objectives], identifying common areas for improvement and standout successes."

3. Analyze Feedback with AI:

   - Use the AI tool to analyze the collected feedback based on your prompts. Let the AI extract and summarize key trends and commonalities.

4. Review and Strategize:

   - Examine the AI-generated summaries for insights into student learning patterns. Note which areas were most frequently cited for improvement and which were highlighted as strengths.

5. Develop Focused Educational Strategies:

   - Create focused educational strategies or interventions based on the AI insights. Aim to reinforce strengths and address common areas of weakness across the cohort.

6. Post-Implementation AI Prompt for Educators:

   - "Generate a follow-up analysis comparing student performance and engagement before and after the implementation of targeted educational strategies based on AI insights."

Through these activities, educators can leverage AI to gain a deeper understanding of their students' learning patterns and needs, enabling them to tailor their teaching approaches more effectively and foster a more supportive learning environment.

5.4 Customizing AI Prompts for Formative and Summative Assessments

Formative and summative assessments are two cornerstone methods of evaluating student learning, each serving unique purposes within the education cycle. Formative assessments are typically conducted during the learning process, offering immediate feedback to both students and teachers about how well the material is being understood, thereby guiding future teaching strategies. Summative assessments, on the other hand, evaluate student learning at the end of an instructional period, measuring their mastery of subject matter against predefined benchmarks.

Integrating AI into both assessment types can enhance their effectiveness and provide more personalized insights. By crafting tailored AI prompts, educators can generate varied and nuanced assessment questions that align closely with learning objectives, ensuring a comprehensive evaluation of student understanding and performance.

Activity 1: AI-Enhanced Formative Assessment Creation

Tools & Materials Needed:

- AI educational tool capable of generating assessment questions

- Access to learning materials and objectives for the current unit

- Digital platform or paper for distributing assessments

Time Needed: 1-2 hours

Outcome: A set of AI-generated formative assessment questions tailored to the current learning objectives, providing insights into student understanding.

Instructions:

1. Review Learning Objectives:

   ○ Clearly identify the learning objectives for the current unit or topic.

2. Develop AI Prompts for Formative Questions:

   ○ Write AI prompts such as "Generate formative assessment questions that check for understanding of [specific learning objectives], suitable for [grade level]."

3. Generate and Review Questions:

- Use the AI tool with your prompts to create a variety of formative assessment questions. Review these questions to ensure they align with your learning objectives and are appropriate for your students.

4. Implement Formative Assessment:

- Distribute the AI-generated questions to your students as part of a class activity, homework, or quiz. Collect their responses for analysis.

5. Analyze Responses and Adapt Instruction:

- Review student responses to identify trends, misconceptions, and areas of strong understanding. Use these insights to adapt your subsequent teaching strategies and materials.

Activity 2: Crafting a Summative Assessment with AI

Tools & Materials Needed:

- AI question-generation tool suitable for educational assessments

- Curriculum standards and learning objectives for the entire unit

- Assessment format template (multiple choice, essay, project, etc.)

Time Needed: 2-3 hours

Outcome: A comprehensive, AI-generated summative assessment that evaluates student mastery of the unit's learning objectives.

Instructions:

1. Summarize Unit Objectives:

- Compile a comprehensive list of the learning objectives covered throughout the unit.

2. Formulate AI Prompts for Summative Assessment:

- Develop AI prompts like "Create summative assessment tasks that measure student mastery of [compiled learning objectives], formatted for [chosen assessment type]."

3. Generate Summative Assessment:

- Input the AI prompts into the educational tool to produce the summative assessment. Ensure the generated assessment covers a broad range of the unit's objectives.

4. Conduct and Evaluate the Assessment:

○ Administer the AI-generated summative assessment to your students. Grade their responses, paying close attention to how well they reflect the stated learning objectives.

5. Reflect on Assessment Outcomes:

○ Analyze the overall performance to gauge the effectiveness of your teaching and the assessment itself. Identify any discrepancies between expected and actual student understanding.

Activity 3: Combining AI with Student Feedback for Assessment Improvement

Tools & Materials Needed:

- AI tool for generating and analyzing feedback questions

- Results from recent formative and summative assessments

- Digital survey tool or paper for collecting student feedback

Time Needed: 1-2 hours

Outcome: Improved assessment strategies informed by AI analysis and student feedback.

Instructions:

1. Gather Recent Assessment Data:

○ Collect data and student responses from recent formative and summative assessments.

2. Create AI Prompts for Feedback Generation:

○ Write AI prompts such as "Generate questions to collect student feedback on the clarity, relevance, and fairness of recent assessments in [subject]."

3. Collect and Analyze Student Feedback:

○ Use the AI-generated questions to create a feedback survey. Distribute this to students and analyze their responses upon completion.

4. Review and Adapt Assessment Practices:

○ Review the student feedback alongside the AI insights. Identify patterns and common issues raised by students regarding the assessments.

5. Implement Changes and Document Impact:

○ Make necessary adjustments to your assessment practices based on the feedback and AI insights. Document any changes made and plan to review the impact of these changes on student performance in future assessments.

6. Post-Implementation AI Prompt for Educators:

○ "Generate an analysis comparing student performance and feedback before and after adjustments were made to the assessment strategies."

Through these activities, educators can effectively utilize AI to enhance both formative and summative assessments, making them more aligned with educational goals and responsive to student needs. This process not only aids in accurately gauging student understanding but also in continually refining teaching and assessment methods for optimal learning outcomes.

5.5 Facilitating Peer Review and Self-Assessment

Peer review and self-assessment are crucial components of a comprehensive educational approach, fostering an environment where students are encouraged to reflect upon and critique their own and others' work constructively. These processes help develop critical thinking and self-regulation skills and promote a deeper understanding of subject matter through collaboration and feedback. Implementing AI in these activities can provide structured, unbiased prompts that guide students to consider specific aspects of their work and the work of their peers in a constructive manner, enhancing the learning experience.

Crafting collaborative AI prompts for peer review and self-assessment involves creating questions or statements that encourage students to reflect on specific elements of a project or assignment. These prompts should be designed to help students give and receive feedback that is insightful, actionable, and conducive to improvement. By integrating AI into this process, educators can ensure that reviews are focused, equitable, and aligned with learning objectives.

Activity 1: AI-Enhanced Peer Review for Writing Assignments

Tools & Materials Needed:

- AI tool capable of generating review questions

- Students' written assignments

- Guidelines for constructive feedback

- Digital platform for exchanging reviews (optional)

Time Needed: 1-2 class periods

Outcome: Enhanced understanding of writing objectives and improved drafts through constructive peer feedback.

Instructions:

1. Explain the Peer Review Process:

   ○ Brief students on the purpose and benefits of peer review. Provide guidelines on giving constructive, respectful feedback.

2. Develop AI Prompts for Peer Review:

   ○ Generate AI prompts such as "Generate specific questions to guide peer review of narrative essays, focusing on plot structure, character development, and use of language."

3. Facilitate Peer Exchange:

   ○ Distribute the AI-generated questions to students along with their peers' essays. If possible, use a digital platform where students can anonymously exchange their work.

4. Conduct Peer Review:

   ○ Students review their assigned essays based on the AI-generated prompts and provide feedback according to the guidelines provided.

5. Reflect and Revise:

   ○ After receiving feedback, students reflect on the comments and revise their essays accordingly. Facilitate a discussion on the review process and its impact.

Activity 2: AI-Prompted Self-Assessment for Projects

Tools & Materials Needed:

- AI tool for generating reflective questions

- Rubric or criteria for the project

- Self-assessment forms or digital questionnaire platform

Time Needed: 1 hour

Outcome: Increased self-awareness and project improvement through guided self-assessment.

Instructions:

1. Introduce Self-Assessment:

- ○ Explain the self-assessment process and its benefits. Distribute the project rubric or criteria to help guide students' reflections.

2. Create AI Self-Assessment Prompts:

- ○ Use AI to generate prompts like "Reflect on your project in relation to the provided rubric. What are the strengths of your project? Where do you see opportunities for improvement?"

3. Conduct Self-Assessment:

- ○ Students complete the self-assessment using the AI-generated prompts, critically analyzing their work against the rubric.

4. Compile and Discuss Findings:

- ○ Students compile their assessments, noting key areas for improvement and strengths. Facilitate a class discussion where students can share their insights and learning experiences.

5. Plan for Revisions:

- ○ Based on the self-assessment, students plan and make revisions to their projects. Provide additional support as needed based on common trends identified in the assessments.

Activity 3: Combined Peer and Self-Assessment for Group Work

Tools & Materials Needed:

- AI tool for creating assessment prompts
- Group project descriptions and objectives
- Feedback and reflection forms

Time Needed: 2 class periods

Outcome: Improved group dynamics and project outcomes through structured peer and self-evaluations.

Instructions:

1. Brief on Assessment Objectives:

- ○ Discuss the goals of peer and self-assessment within the context of group work. Clarify expectations for constructive feedback and self-reflection.

2. Generate AI Assessment Prompts:

- Develop AI prompts such as "List key aspects to evaluate in a group project, including collaboration, contribution, and adherence to objectives" for peer review and "Reflect on your contribution and learning in the group project" for self-assessment.

3. Facilitate Assessment Sessions:

- Students first complete self-assessments using the AI-generated prompts. Then, they use another set of AI-generated prompts to provide feedback on their group members' contributions and the project as a whole.

4. Review and Share Feedback:

- In a controlled environment, allow students to share and discuss the feedback received. Guide the conversation to ensure it remains constructive and focused on project improvement.

5. Implement Changes and Reflect:

- Groups discuss the feedback and identify actionable changes to improve their work and group dynamics. Conclude with a reflection on the overall process and its impact on their projects and teamwork skills.

6. Post-Implementation AI Prompt for Educators:

- "Generate questions for students to reflect on the efficacy of the peer and self-assessment process in enhancing their understanding and performance in group projects."

These activities encourage a culture of continuous improvement and collaboration among students, fostering not only academic growth but also interpersonal and self-reflective skills. By incorporating AI-generated prompts, educators can facilitate more focused, relevant, and constructive peer and self-assessment experiences.

Chapter Six

Prompts for Curriculum Development

6.1 Utilizing AI for Curriculum Mapping

Curriculum mapping is an essential process in educational planning, serving to align curriculum with educational standards and ensuring logical progression of content across different subjects and grade levels. The use of AI in this process can significantly enhance efficiency, coherence, and alignment, allowing educators to create more integrated and comprehensive curriculum maps. AI can analyze vast amounts of educational data, identify connections between different learning objectives and standards, and suggest logical sequences for content delivery.

By leveraging AI for curriculum mapping, educators can ensure that all necessary standards are covered and that the learning objectives are met in an organized manner. This technology can help identify gaps in the curriculum, redundancies, and misalignments, providing opportunities for improvement and adjustment. Moreover, AI-generated curriculum maps can be easily updated and modified, allowing for flexibility and ongoing refinement to meet the evolving needs of students and educational standards.

Crafting AI prompts for curriculum mapping involves asking the right questions to generate a curriculum that aligns learning objectives with the necessary standards, logically sequences the content, and integrates across different subjects where applicable. Educators can utilize these AI-generated maps to streamline their planning processes, enhance interdisciplinary connections, and ensure that their teaching is standards-aligned and comprehensive.

Activity 1: Creating an AI-Generated Curriculum Map for Science

Tools & Materials Needed:

- AI curriculum mapping tool

- State or national science standards

- Current science curriculum documents

Time Needed: 2-3 hours

Outcome: An AI-generated curriculum map for science, aligned with educational standards.

Instructions:

1. Gather Resources:

   - Compile the current science curriculum documents and the relevant state or national standards.

2. Develop AI Mapping Prompts:

   - Construct AI prompts such as "Generate a curriculum map for grade [specific grade] science that aligns with [specific standards], ensuring a logical progression of topics and integration of key skills."

3. Generate Curriculum Map:

   - Input the AI prompts into the curriculum mapping tool. Review the generated curriculum map, focusing on coverage of standards, logical sequencing, and thematic connections.

4. Compare and Analyze:

   - Compare the AI-generated curriculum map with the existing curriculum. Identify areas of improvement, gaps, or redundancies.

5. Refine and Implement:

   - Make adjustments to the AI-generated map based on your analysis. Plan to integrate these changes into the actual teaching schedule.

Activity 2: Interdisciplinary Curriculum Mapping with AI

Tools & Materials Needed:

- AI curriculum mapping software

- Educational standards for multiple subjects

- Current curriculum documents for those subjects

Time Needed: 3-4 hours

Outcome: A comprehensive, AI-generated interdisciplinary curriculum map.

Instructions:

1. Collect Curriculum Documents and Standards:

    ○ Gather existing curriculum documents and educational standards for the subjects you wish to integrate.

2. Formulate AI Mapping Prompts:

    ○ Write AI prompts like "Create an interdisciplinary curriculum map that aligns grade [specific grade] English and History standards, highlighting thematic connections and opportunities for collaborative projects."

3. Initiate AI Mapping Process:

    ○ Enter the AI prompts into the mapping software. Analyze the generated map for interdisciplinary links, coherence, and alignment with standards.

4. Evaluate and Cross-Reference:

    ○ Compare the AI-generated map with current curriculum plans. Note new connections, overlaps, and potential collaborative learning opportunities.

5. Adjust and Plan for Application:

    ○ Adapt the interdisciplinary curriculum map based on your findings. Outline a plan for integrating these connections into upcoming lessons or units.

Activity 3: Evaluating and Revising Social Studies Curriculum with AI

Tools & Materials Needed:

- AI mapping tool

- Current Social Studies curriculum and standards

- Feedback from previous implementations (surveys, test results)

Time Needed: 2-3 hours

Outcome: An updated, AI-enhanced curriculum map for Social Studies, addressing previous gaps and incorporating feedback.

Instructions:

1. Prepare Existing Materials and Feedback:

   - Review your current Social Studies curriculum alongside educational standards and feedback from prior implementations.

2. Craft AI Prompts for Curriculum Revision:

   - Develop AI prompts such as "Revise the current Social Studies curriculum map for [specific grade] to better address historical thinking skills and incorporate feedback on student engagement and understanding."

3. Generate Revised Curriculum Map:

   - Use the AI curriculum mapping tool with your prompts to produce a revised curriculum map. Focus on areas highlighted by feedback and standards alignment.

4. Analyze and Compare:

   - Analyze the revised AI-generated curriculum map. Compare it with the original to identify significant changes, improvements, and areas needing further revision.

5. Implement and Monitor:

   - Implement the revised curriculum plan. Set up mechanisms to monitor its effectiveness and gather ongoing feedback for future adjustments.

6. Post-Implementation AI Prompt for Educators:

   - "Generate follow-up questions to assess the effectiveness and reception of the revised Social Studies curriculum among students and educators, focusing on engagement, understanding, and skills development."

By engaging in these activities, educators can effectively utilize AI to enhance their curriculum mapping processes, ensuring that their teaching is not only standards-aligned but also responsive to student needs and feedback. This approach facilitates a more structured, coherent, and integrated educational experience for students.

6.2 Identifying and Filling Curriculum Gaps

Ensuring that a curriculum is comprehensive and balanced is crucial for providing a quality education that addresses all necessary educational standards and meets diverse student needs. However, identifying gaps within an existing curriculum can be a complex and time-consuming process. Integrating AI into this task can streamline the process, enabling educators to conduct a thorough analysis of their curricula against established standards and learning goals, thereby identifying any gaps or redundancies more efficiently.

Using AI, educators can receive data-driven insights into areas where the curriculum may lack comprehensive coverage or where it might not align perfectly with the required standards. This process not only saves time but also provides a more objective analysis, helping educators make informed decisions about where to adjust their curricula. The ultimate goal is to ensure that all students have access to a well-rounded education that prepares them for future challenges and opportunities.

Interactive AI prompts can be specifically designed to aid educators in this analysis, helping them identify areas that require additional content, different instructional strategies, or enhanced resources. By leveraging AI in this way, educators can ensure their curricula are fully aligned with educational standards and are effectively meeting students' learning needs.

Activity 1: AI-Assisted Analysis of Math Curriculum

Tools & Materials Needed:

- AI curriculum analysis tool

- Current math curriculum documents

- Applicable math standards (state or national)

Time Needed: 2-3 hours

Outcome: A detailed report identifying gaps in the current math curriculum and suggestions to fill these gaps.

Instructions:

1. Prepare Curriculum Documents and Standards:

   ○ Gather your current math curriculum and the relevant educational standards. Ensure all documents are in a format compatible with your AI analysis tool.

2. Develop AI Analysis Prompts:

   ○ Construct AI prompts like "Compare the current math curriculum for grade [specific grade] against [specific standards]. Highlight areas where the curriculum does not meet the standards or appears lacking in content."

3. Run AI Analysis:

   ○ Input your curriculum documents and standards into the AI tool along with the analysis prompts. Allow the AI to process and analyze the data.

4. Review AI Findings:

○ Examine the AI-generated report to identify any noted gaps or areas of redundancy within your current math curriculum.

5. Plan Curriculum Adjustments:

○ Based on the AI findings, plan adjustments or additions to the math curriculum to address identified gaps. Consider incorporating suggested resources or activities provided by the AI.

Activity 2: Filling Gaps in Science Curriculum Using AI

Tools & Materials Needed:

- AI curriculum evaluation software

- Current science curriculum and state or national standards

- List of learning objectives for the science course

Time Needed: 3-4 hours

Outcome: Updated science curriculum with gaps filled based on AI recommendations.

Instructions:

1. Organize Curriculum and Standards:

○ Collect your science curriculum materials and align them with the corresponding educational standards and learning objectives.

2. Formulate AI Evaluation Prompts:

○ Create prompts for the AI such as "Identify discrepancies between the provided science curriculum and the associated standards for grade [specific grade], focusing on areas such as environmental science and physical sciences."

3. Execute AI Evaluation:

○ Use the AI tool to analyze the curriculum against the standards with your prompts. Let the AI identify where the curriculum falls short or exceeds necessary standards.

4. Analyze Results and Identify Gaps:

○ Review the outcomes highlighted by the AI, noting particularly where the curriculum lacks coverage or depth.

5. Implement AI Recommendations:

○ Utilize the AI's suggestions to fill in the gaps in the science curriculum. This may involve adding new units, expanding existing lessons, or integrating new instructional resources.

Activity 3: Enhancing English Curriculum with AI Insights

Tools & Materials Needed:

- AI tool for curriculum mapping and analysis

- English curriculum documentation

- English language arts standards

Time Needed: 2-3 hours

Outcome: An enhanced English curriculum that addresses previously unidentified gaps as per AI analysis.

Instructions:

1. Collect Curriculum Materials and Standards:

   ○ Assemble all materials related to the English curriculum and the relevant educational standards for language arts.

2. Generate AI Analysis Prompts:

   ○ Write prompts for the AI such as "Analyze the English curriculum for [grade level] to uncover gaps in literary analysis, writing skills, and vocabulary development as compared to [specified standards]."

3. Conduct the AI Curriculum Analysis:

   ○ Input the curriculum materials and standards into the AI analysis tool. Process the data using your custom prompts.

4. Review AI Analysis for Curriculum Gaps:

   ○ Examine the AI's report to pinpoint areas where the English curriculum may be lacking or misaligned with the standards.

5. Update Curriculum Based on AI Feedback:

   ○ Adapt the English curriculum to fill in the identified gaps, incorporating AI-suggested content, activities, and assessment strategies.

6. Post-Implementation AI Prompt for Educators:

   ○ "Generate a follow-up survey for students and teachers to evaluate the changes made to the English curriculum and measure improvements in student understanding and skills."

By following these activities, educators can leverage AI to conduct thorough curriculum analyses, identify and address gaps, and ensure that their teaching is fully aligned with educational standards, ultimately leading to a richer, more comprehensive learning experience for students.

6.3 Enhancing Curriculum Content with AI

In the rapidly evolving educational landscape, the incorporation of diverse, current, and relevant resources into the curriculum is essential for maintaining student interest and engagement. Today's students benefit from content that reflects the latest developments in various fields and connects with their experiences and interests. AI can play a pivotal role in this process by suggesting updated resources, interactive activities, and innovative teaching materials that cater to a wide range of learning styles and preferences.

Creating AI prompts for enhancing curriculum content involves asking the AI to suggest materials and activities based on specific topics, trends, and student demographics. These AI-generated solutions can provide educators with fresh ideas and approaches, helping to bring new life to traditional subjects and making learning more relevant and engaging for students. By aligning these resources with educational standards and learning objectives, educators can ensure that their curriculum remains dynamic and comprehensive.

Using AI to enhance curriculum content not only saves educators time and effort but also ensures that the educational material is diverse, inclusive, and aligned with the real world. This approach encourages a more holistic and adaptable learning environment where students can see the direct application of their studies to real-world scenarios, thereby increasing their motivation and engagement.

Activity 1: Updating a History Lesson Plan with AI Suggestions

Tools & Materials Needed:

- AI tool capable of suggesting educational resources

- Current history lesson plan and educational standards

- Access to digital platforms for research and content sharing

Time Needed: 2-3 hours

Outcome: A revised history lesson plan enriched with AI-suggested resources and activities, leading to increased student engagement.

Instructions:

1. Select a Lesson Plan for Revision:

   ○ Choose a history lesson plan that could benefit from updated materials and new teaching methods.

2. Generate AI Resource Prompts:

   ○ Create AI prompts such as "Suggest modern resources and interactive activities for a lesson on [specific historical topic], tailored to [grade level] students with diverse interests."

3. Collect AI-Generated Suggestions:

   ○ Input your prompts into the AI tool and collect the suggested resources, such as digital archives, interactive timelines, or current articles that relate to the lesson's topic.

4. Revise the Lesson Plan:

   ○ Incorporate the AI-suggested materials into your lesson plan. Update learning objectives, activities, and assessment methods to align with the new content.

5. Implement and Evaluate:

   ○ Teach the updated lesson to your class. Afterward, assess student engagement and understanding compared to previous iterations of the lesson.

Activity 2: Enhancing Math Curriculum with AI-Generated Interactive Tools

Tools & Materials Needed:

- AI recommendation tool for educational materials

- Current math curriculum outline

- Devices or software to access and implement interactive math tools

Time Needed: 3-4 hours

Outcome: An enriched math curriculum incorporating AI-recommended interactive tools and activities.

Instructions:

1. Identify Areas for Enhancement:

   ○ Review your current math curriculum to identify topics that could be enhanced with interactive tools or new methodologies.

2. Develop AI Enhancement Prompts:

   ○ Write AI prompts such as "Identify interactive math tools and resources that facilitate understanding of [math concept] for [specific grade level], focusing on real-world application and student engagement."

3. Gather and Review AI Suggestions:

   ○ Use the AI tool to obtain recommendations. Review the suggested interactive tools and resources for suitability and alignment with curriculum goals.

4. Integrate New Resources into Curriculum:

   ○ Select the most appropriate AI-recommended tools and activities. Update your curriculum to include these resources, detailing how and when they will be used.

5. Monitor and Assess Impact:

   ○ Implement the updated curriculum sections and monitor student response and performance. Collect feedback to gauge the effectiveness of the new tools and activities.

Activity 3: Reinvigorating Science Lessons with Current Events and AI Insights

Tools & Materials Needed:

- AI tool for curating content related to current events

- Science lesson plans in need of updates

- Access to multimedia resources and platforms

Time Needed: 2-3 hours

Outcome: Updated science lesson plans that incorporate current events and AI-suggested resources, increasing relevance and student interest.

Instructions:

1. Select Science Topics for Update:

   ○ Choose specific topics within your science curriculum that could be enhanced by relating them to current events or discoveries.

2. Craft AI Prompts for Current Event Integration:

   ○ Develop AI prompts such as "Provide recent articles, studies, and multimedia resources related to [science topic] that can be integrated into a lesson plan for [grade level]."

3. Retrieve and Evaluate AI Recommendations:

- Input the prompts into the AI tool and collect the generated resources. Evaluate their relevance, accuracy, and educational value.

4. Revise Lesson Plans:

- Incorporate the selected resources into your lesson plans. Adjust the content, activities, and assessments to reflect the new information and resources.

5. Implement, Monitor, and Reflect:

- Teach the revised lessons and monitor student reactions and learning outcomes. Reflect on the integration process and student feedback to inform future curriculum enhancements.

6. Post-Implementation AI Prompt for Educators:

- "Generate a template for students to provide feedback on the updated lesson content, focusing on engagement, relevance, and understanding of the science topics."

By implementing these activities, educators can leverage AI to bring fresh perspectives and resources into their curriculum, making the learning experience more engaging, relevant, and effective for students.

6.4 Personalizing Learning Paths within the Curriculum

The concept of personalized learning paths represents a shift from a one-size-fits-all approach to an educational model that respects and accommodates the diverse learning styles, paces, and interests of individual students. Personalized learning paths allow educators to meet students where they are, providing tailored educational experiences that promote deeper understanding, increase engagement, and foster independent learning skills. By utilizing AI, educators can analyze student data, preferences, and performance to create differentiated learning experiences that align with the broader curriculum framework, ensuring all students have the opportunity to succeed according to their own terms.

Custom AI prompts can be specifically designed to aid in this process, guiding the AI in generating suggestions for materials, activities, and assessments that cater to the individual needs and goals of different student groups. This approach not only streamlines the creation of personalized learning paths but also ensures they are rooted in sound educational practices and aligned with overarching learning objectives.

By integrating personalized learning paths into the curriculum, educators can provide a more adaptive and responsive learning environment. This approach not only supports students in achieving their personal learning goals but also prepares them for the challenges of the real world, where flexibility, critical thinking, and self-directed learning are invaluable skills.

Activity 1: Differentiated Learning Paths for Math Mastery

Tools & Materials Needed:

- AI tool capable of analyzing student performance and generating learning recommendations

- Current math curriculum framework and standards

- Student performance data and learning style assessments

Time Needed: 3-4 hours

Outcome: A set of personalized learning paths for a math unit, designed to cater to the varying needs and abilities of students.

Instructions:

1. Assess Student Needs and Abilities:

   - Collect and review recent math performance data for your class, along with any available information on individual learning styles or preferences.

2. Generate AI Prompts for Personalized Paths:

   - Develop AI prompts like "Create differentiated learning paths for students based on their performance data and learning styles, focusing on [specific math concepts or units]."

3. Implement AI Recommendations:

   - Input the student data and AI prompts into the tool. Review the AI-generated learning paths, ensuring they align with curriculum standards and address individual student needs.

4. Integrate Personalized Paths into Curriculum:

   - Adjust your existing math curriculum to incorporate the personalized learning paths. This may involve creating tiered assignments, offering various resource types, or allowing students to choose among different activity options.

5. Monitor Progress and Adjust as Necessary:

○ Implement the differentiated learning paths in your classroom. Monitor student progress and engagement, making adjustments based on feedback and performance.

Activity 2: Tailoring English Literature Studies to Student Interests

Tools & Materials Needed:

- AI recommendation system for educational content

- List of English literature themes, genres, and reading materials

- Surveys or questionnaires on student interests and reading preferences

Time Needed: 2-3 hours

Outcome: Customized English literature study segments that align with students' interests and learning goals.

Instructions:

1. Gather Student Interests and Preferences:

   ○ Conduct a survey to gather information on your students' literary interests, preferred genres, and reading habits.

2. Craft AI Prompts for Custom Content:

   ○ Write AI prompts such as "Suggest literary works and corresponding activities that match the interests of students grouped by [specific preferences or genres]."

3. Generate and Review AI Suggestions:

   ○ Use the AI tool to generate suggestions based on student interests. Review the recommended literary works and activities for suitability and alignment with learning objectives.

4. Design Personalized Literature Studies:

   ○ Create tailored literature study segments for different student groups based on AI suggestions. Include varied activities and discussion topics that cater to different interests and learning styles.

5. Implement and Reflect:

   ○ Introduce the personalized literature studies in your curriculum. After completion, collect student feedback and reflect on the effectiveness of the personalized approach.

Activity 3: Creating Individualized Science Exploration Projects

Tools & Materials Needed:

- AI curriculum development tool

- Science curriculum goals and standards

- Inventory of student science interests and current understanding levels

Time Needed: 3-4 hours

Outcome: Individualized science exploration projects tailored to student interests and existing knowledge levels.

Instructions:

1. Identify Student Interests and Knowledge:

   - Review assessments of student interests and understanding in various science topics to identify starting points for individualized projects.

2. Generate AI Learning Path Prompts:

   - Formulate AI prompts like "Develop personalized science exploration projects for students based on their individual interests in [list of science topics] and current understanding levels."

3. Use AI to Design Exploration Projects:

   - Input your prompts into the AI tool. Review the generated project ideas for relevance to student interests and appropriateness for their knowledge levels.

4. Assign and Guide Projects:

   - Assign the AI-generated exploration projects to students. Provide guidance and resources to support their independent research and project development.

5. Review and Share Outcomes:

   - Have students present their exploration projects. Evaluate the projects based on science standards and personal learning growth, and encourage peer feedback.

6. Post-Implementation AI Prompt for Educators:

   - "Generate follow-up questions to assess student engagement and learning outcomes from the personalized science exploration projects."

Through these activities, educators can effectively use AI to create personalized learning experiences within the curriculum, allowing students to engage more deeply with the material and pursue their individual learning goals. This approach not only enhances student motivation and satisfaction but also promotes a deeper, more meaningful understanding of the subject matter.

6.5 Collaborating on Curriculum Development using AI

In the realm of education, collaboration among educators is key to developing a cohesive and comprehensive curriculum that addresses the diverse needs of students. AI technology has the potential to significantly enhance this collaborative process, offering tools that can streamline the sharing, reviewing, and integrating of various curriculum components. By utilizing AI, educators can efficiently merge their individual expertise and insights, leading to a more unified and effective educational program.

AI prompts specifically tailored for collaborative curriculum development can assist educators in identifying areas of overlap, gaps, or inconsistencies across different curriculum contributions. These prompts can guide the AI in suggesting adjustments, alignments, and enhancements, ensuring that the final curriculum is well-rounded and adheres to educational standards. By facilitating a smoother integration of diverse educational content, AI helps maintain a clear and consistent learning pathway for students, irrespective of the number of educators involved in the curriculum development process.

The use of AI in this collaborative endeavor not only saves time but also fosters a more productive and harmonious environment among educators. It allows for the seamless merging of various perspectives and specialties, enhancing the curriculum with a rich tapestry of knowledge and teaching approaches. This collaborative approach, augmented by AI, ensures that the curriculum not only meets educational standards but also reflects the collective wisdom and expertise of the entire teaching team.

Activity 1: Joint Curriculum Mapping with AI Assistance

Tools & Materials Needed:

- AI-powered curriculum mapping tool

- Access to the current curriculum outlines from each participating educator

- Standards and benchmarks relevant to the subject area or grade level

Time Needed: 3-4 hours

Outcome: A unified curriculum map developed collaboratively by educators, enhanced by AI-generated suggestions for cohesion and coverage.

Instructions:

1. Collect and Compile Curriculum Contributions:

   ○ Each educator submits their portion of the curriculum outline, highlighting key concepts, objectives, and resources they've developed or used.

2. Generate AI Collaboration Prompts:

   ○ Develop AI prompts such as "Integrate these separate curriculum outlines into a unified map, ensuring alignment with [specified standards] and continuity across topics."

3. Run the AI Integration Process:

   ○ Use the AI tool with the provided prompts to merge the individual curriculum contributions. Review the integrated curriculum map generated by the AI.

4. Discuss and Refine Collaboratively:

   ○ Organize a session where all contributing educators review the AI-integrated curriculum map. Discuss and make collective decisions on any adjustments needed to ensure clarity, flow, and comprehensive coverage.

5. Finalize and Implement the Unified Curriculum:

   ○ Apply agreed-upon changes and finalize the collaborative curriculum map. Plan for implementation and monitoring of the new integrated curriculum.

Activity 2: Collaborative Unit Development Workshop using AI

Tools & Materials Needed:

- AI curriculum development platform

- Individual unit plans or materials from participating educators

- Digital workspace for collaborative editing

Time Needed: 4-5 hours

Outcome: A cohesively developed educational unit that incorporates the expertise and materials of multiple educators, refined with AI support.

Instructions:

1. Prepare and Share Individual Unit Plans:

- Each educator prepares a draft of their unit plan, including objectives, activities, assessments, and resources.

2. Craft AI Synthesis Prompts:

- Write AI prompts like "Synthesize these individual unit plans into a coherent educational unit, identifying and incorporating the most effective elements from each."

3. Conduct AI-Assisted Synthesis:

- Input the unit plans and AI prompts into the platform. Review the synthesized unit draft generated by the AI for coherence and inclusivity of diverse educational approaches.

4. Collaborative Editing and Enhancement:

- In a workshop setting, educators collaboratively review and edit the AI-suggested unit, ensuring that it meets collective goals and leverages individual strengths.

5. Consolidation and Application:

- Finalize the unit plan incorporating all agreed changes. Set a schedule for implementing the new unit and collecting feedback on its effectiveness.

Activity 3: AI-Facilitated Review and Feedback Cycle

Tools & Materials Needed:

- AI feedback tool for educational content

- Curriculum documents or units developed by the educator team

- Criteria for curriculum evaluation and feedback

Time Needed: 3-4 hours

Outcome: A refined curriculum or unit that has been collaboratively reviewed and improved based on AI-generated feedback and peer insights.

Instructions:

1. Compile Curriculum Documents for Review:

- Gather the latest versions of the curriculum or unit documents developed collaboratively by the educator team.

2. Initiate AI Feedback Prompts:

- Develop prompts for the AI tool such as "Provide detailed feedback on this collaborative curriculum, focusing on alignment with learning goals, interdisciplinary connections, and learner engagement."

3. Engage in AI-Assisted Feedback Process:

- Submit the curriculum documents to the AI feedback tool. Distribute the AI-generated feedback among the educator team for review.

4. Organize a Collaborative Feedback Session:

- Hold a session where educators discuss the AI feedback, share personal insights, and propose revisions based on collective expertise and AI suggestions.

5. Revise and Enhance the Curriculum:

- Incorporate the agreed-upon changes into the curriculum. Plan a follow-up session to evaluate the implementation and impact of the revised content.

6. Post-Implementation AI Prompt for Educators:

- "Generate a set of questions to guide a post-implementation review of the newly developed curriculum, focusing on areas such as student engagement, learning outcomes, and interdisciplinary integration."

By engaging in these activities, educators can effectively utilize AI to foster a collaborative environment for curriculum development, resulting in educational content that is rich, diverse, and attuned to the needs of all students. This collaborative approach, enhanced by AI insights, ensures that the curriculum is not only comprehensive and standards-aligned but also reflective of the collective expertise of the educational team.

Chapter Seven

Prompts for Professional Development

7.1 Self-Assessment and Growth Planning

Self-assessment is a critical component of professional development, particularly in the field of education. It enables educators to reflect on their teaching practices, methodologies, and content knowledge critically. By engaging in self-assessment, educators can identify areas of strength and opportunities for growth, leading to targeted and effective professional development. Integrating AI into this process can enhance the depth and objectivity of self-assessments, providing educators with unbiased, data-driven insights into their teaching practices.

Crafting AI prompts for self-assessment involves asking the right questions to guide educators through a comprehensive evaluation of their professional skills and knowledge areas. These prompts can help uncover aspects of their teaching that may benefit from further development or refinement. AI can analyze responses to these prompts against best practices and educational standards, offering a unique perspective on the educator's performance and potential growth areas.

By using AI-generated prompts for self-assessment, educators can develop a more nuanced understanding of their teaching effectiveness. This process not only aids in personal reflection but also in the creation of a personalized professional growth plan. Such a plan, informed by AI insights, can be more aligned with the educator's specific needs and goals, leading to more meaningful and impactful professional development.

Activity 1: AI-Assisted Self-Assessment of Teaching Practices

Tools & Materials Needed:

- AI tool capable of generating and analyzing self-assessment prompts

- Access to teaching evaluations, student feedback, and personal teaching records

- Template for a professional growth plan

Time Needed: 2-3 hours

Outcome: A comprehensive self-assessment of teaching practices and a personalized professional growth plan.

Instructions:

1. Collect and Review Personal Teaching Data:

   ○ Gather your recent teaching evaluations, student feedback, and examples of lesson plans or recorded teaching sessions.

2. Develop AI Self-Assessment Prompts:

   ○ Craft AI prompts such as "Analyze my teaching evaluations and generate a detailed self-assessment report focusing on areas such as classroom management, student engagement, and instructional strategies."

3. Conduct the AI-Assisted Self-Assessment:

   ○ Input your teaching data and the AI prompts into the tool. Review the AI-generated self-assessment report, noting areas highlighted for improvement and strengths.

4. Develop a Personalized Professional Growth Plan:

   ○ Based on the AI insights, outline a professional growth plan addressing identified areas for improvement and strategies to enhance your teaching strengths.

5. Implement, Monitor, and Adjust the Growth Plan:

   ○ Begin implementing the strategies outlined in your growth plan. Regularly monitor your progress and adjust the plan as necessary based on further reflection and feedback.

Activity 2: Evaluating Content Knowledge with AI

Tools & Materials Needed:

- AI educational platform with content knowledge assessment capabilities

- List of curriculum topics or standards for self-assessment

- Framework for a professional development plan

Time Needed: 1-2 hours

Outcome: An AI-driven evaluation of content knowledge and a targeted plan for enhancing subject matter expertise.

Instructions:

1. Select Topics for Assessment:

   ○ Choose key topics or standards from your teaching area that you wish to assess for your content knowledge.

2. Create AI Evaluation Prompts:

   ○ Formulate AI prompts like "Evaluate my understanding of [selected topics] and suggest areas for deeper learning and improvement."

3. Run the AI Content Knowledge Evaluation:

   ○ Input the selected topics and AI prompts into the educational platform. Engage with the AI-generated assessment activities and review your results.

4. Formulate a Subject Matter Improvement Plan:

   ○ Based on the AI assessment results, develop a plan focused on enhancing your understanding and teaching of the identified topics.

5. Apply and Reflect on the Improvement Plan:

   ○ Implement the strategies identified in your improvement plan. Reflect on changes in your teaching efficacy and student responses as you enhance your content knowledge.

Activity 3: Refining Instructional Strategies with AI Insights

Tools & Materials Needed:

- AI tool for instructional strategy feedback

- Samples of lesson plans, teaching materials, and student work

- Professional growth planning template

Time Needed: 2-3 hours

Outcome: Insightful feedback on instructional strategies and a detailed action plan for teaching improvement.

Instructions:

1. Gather Teaching Materials for Review:

   ○ Compile a selection of your lesson plans, teaching materials, and examples of student work or outcomes.

2. Generate AI Feedback Prompts:

   ○ Develop AI prompts such as "Provide feedback on these instructional materials and strategies, identifying strengths and recommending areas for development."

3. Engage with the AI for Instructional Feedback:

   ○ Use the AI tool to analyze your teaching materials with the provided prompts. Carefully review the feedback focusing on suggested areas for improvement.

4. Craft a Strategy Enhancement Plan:

   ○ Utilize the AI feedback to create a plan aimed at refining your instructional strategies. Include specific actions, resources, and timelines.

5. Implement, Track, and Adjust Based on Feedback:

   ○ Apply the changes outlined in your enhancement plan to your teaching practice. Regularly assess the impact of these changes and adjust your strategies based on student feedback and outcomes.

6. Post-Implementation AI Prompt for Educators:

   ○ "Generate follow-up evaluation questions to assess the effectiveness of changes made to my instructional strategies and their impact on student learning and engagement."

Through these activities, educators can leverage AI to gain deeper insights into their teaching practices, content knowledge, and instructional strategies. This process not only facilitates personal and professional growth but also contributes to a more effective and engaging learning environment for students.

7.2 Collaborative Learning and Mentoring

Collaborative learning and mentoring among educators play a pivotal role in professional development, fostering a supportive learning community where knowledge, strategies, and experiences are shared. This environment not only enhances individual teaching skills but also contributes to a collective rise in educational quality. The benefits of such collaboration include diverse perspectives, shared resources, mutual support, and a sense of camaraderie that can transform the educational landscape.

Integrating AI into collaborative learning and mentoring can streamline the identification of development opportunities, match mentors with mentees based on complementary needs and skills, and provide structured prompts that guide meaningful interactions and reflections. AI-generated prompts can facilitate focused discussions, reflective practices, and effective goal-setting, ensuring that collaborative activities are purposeful and aligned with professional development objectives.

By fostering a culture of collaborative learning and mentoring, educators can create a dynamic professional community that is continuously evolving. AI aids in this process by offering personalized, data-driven insights and suggestions, making collaborative professional development more impactful and aligned with each educator's unique needs and the collective goals of the educational community.

Activity 1: AI-Facilitated Peer Observation Cycle

Tools & Materials Needed:

- AI tool capable of generating observation prompts and feedback questions

- Digital platform for scheduling observations and sharing feedback

- Guidelines for constructive observation and feedback

Time Needed: One week

Outcome: Enhanced teaching practices through structured peer observations and feedback, facilitated by AI-generated prompts.

Instructions:

1. Pair Educators for Peer Observations:

   ○ Pair educators based on complementary strengths and areas for development. Consider using AI to help make these pairings based on past performance data and professional development goals.

2. Generate AI Observation Prompts:

   ○ Develop AI prompts such as "Create a list of observation focuses for a math class that encourages active student engagement and conceptual understanding."

3. Conduct Peer Observations:

   ○ Schedule and conduct classroom observations based on the AI-generated prompts. Observers should note instances where the focus areas are effectively addressed, as well as opportunities for growth.

4. Share and Discuss Feedback:

- Use the AI tool to generate constructive feedback questions, then share and discuss the feedback in a supportive setting, focusing on growth and improvement.

5. Reflect and Plan for Implementation:

- Both the observer and the observed educator reflect on the feedback and plan specific strategies for implementing the suggestions into their teaching practices.

Activity 2: Developing Mentorship Goals with AI Assistance

Tools & Materials Needed:

- AI platform for mentorship pairing and goal setting

- Access to professional development records and preferences

- Framework for setting and tracking mentorship goals

Time Needed: 2 hours

Outcome: Clearly defined mentorship goals and plans, created with AI assistance, to guide effective mentoring relationships.

Instructions:

1. Pair Mentors and Mentees:

- Use the AI platform to pair mentors and mentees based on areas of expertise, development needs, and professional interests.

2. Generate AI Mentorship Goals:

- Create AI prompts like "Suggest targeted goals for a mentorship relationship focused on improving classroom management techniques for new teachers."

3. Set and Refine Mentorship Goals:

- Use the AI-generated suggestions to establish clear, achievable goals for the mentorship. Mentors and mentees should discuss and refine these goals to ensure they are personalized and relevant.

4. Develop Action Plans:

- Collaboratively develop action plans detailing steps, resources, and timelines for achieving the set goals, utilizing AI tools for additional suggestions and resources.

5. Monitor Progress and Adjust Goals:

- ○ Regularly review progress towards the goals, using AI to generate follow-up questions and adjustments. Reflect on learning and adjust the goals and plans as needed.

Activity 3: AI-Enhanced Group Professional Development Sessions

Tools & Materials Needed:

- AI system for generating group activity prompts

- Digital or physical space for group meetings

- Materials for documenting goals, insights, and follow-up actions

Time Needed: 3 hours

Outcome: Actionable insights and strategies developed through AI-enhanced collaborative professional development sessions.

Instructions:

1. Organize Group Sessions:

- ○ Form small groups of educators with similar professional development interests or needs.

2. Craft AI Collaboration Prompts:

- ○ Use AI to generate prompts such as "Identify key discussion topics and activities that foster collaborative problem-solving in inclusive education practices."

3. Engage in AI-Prompted Activities:

- ○ Conduct the group sessions using the AI-generated prompts to guide discussions, activities, and collaborative problem-solving.

4. Document Insights and Strategies:

- ○ Throughout the session, document key insights, strategies, and action plans developed collaboratively by the group.

5. Plan for Implementation and Follow-up:

- ○ End the session by outlining specific steps each educator will take to implement the strategies in their classrooms. Schedule a follow-up session to review progress and refine approaches based on experience.

6. Post-Implementation AI Prompt for Educators:

   ○ "Generate reflection questions to evaluate the impact of implemented strategies from the group professional development sessions on teaching effectiveness and student learning outcomes."

Through these activities, educators engage in meaningful collaborative learning experiences, guided by AI-generated prompts that ensure relevance and focus. This approach enhances the professional development process, making it more targeted, collaborative, and reflective, ultimately leading to improved teaching practices and student outcomes.

7.3 Staying Updated with Educational Trends

In the dynamic field of education, staying updated with the latest trends, research, and technological advancements is crucial for educators seeking to provide the most effective and relevant learning experiences. Continuous learning and adaptation to new educational strategies and tools not only enhance teaching effectiveness but also ensure that students benefit from the most current and evidence-based approaches. As the educational landscape evolves, so too must educators evolve their practices to meet the changing needs and expectations of their students.

AI technology offers a powerful solution for educators striving to stay current with educational trends. By crafting specific AI prompts, educators can streamline the process of finding and reviewing the latest research, teaching methods, and technological innovations in education. This can significantly reduce the time and effort required to sift through vast amounts of information, allowing educators to quickly access relevant and impactful insights.

Utilizing AI in this way enables educators to remain at the forefront of educational developments, equipping them with the knowledge and tools necessary to continuously improve their teaching and better serve their students. By integrating current educational trends and research findings into their practice, educators can foster a more engaging, effective, and forward-thinking learning environment.

Activity 1: Curating Recent Educational Research with AI

Tools & Materials Needed:

- Access to an AI-powered research curation tool

- Criteria or topics of interest in education

- Digital notetaking tool or journal for reflections

Time Needed: 2 hours

Outcome: A collection of recent educational research articles and a reflective journal entry on potential classroom applications.

Instructions:

> 1. Identify Focus Areas:
>
>> ○ Determine specific areas of interest or current challenges in your teaching practice that could benefit from recent research insights.
>
> 2. Generate AI Research Curation Prompts:
>
>> ○ Formulate AI prompts like "Curate recent educational research articles focused on [specific focus area], highlighting findings relevant to secondary education practices."
>
> 3. Conduct AI-Assisted Research Curation:
>
>> ○ Input your prompts into the AI curation tool. Review the list of suggested articles, selecting those that are most relevant and insightful.
>
> 4. Reflect on Research Findings:
>
>> ○ Read the selected articles, taking notes on key findings, methodologies, and conclusions. Reflect on how these insights could be integrated into your current teaching practices.
>
> 5. Journal Your Reflections and Plans:
>
>> ○ Write a reflective journal entry summarizing the research insights and outlining potential applications or changes to your teaching approach.

Activity 2: Exploring New Teaching Methods via AI

Tools & Materials Needed:

- AI tool capable of aggregating educational content

- Criteria for innovative teaching methods or areas for instructional improvement

- Template for lesson planning and experimentation

Time Needed: 3 hours

Outcome: A set of innovative teaching methods tailored to your educational context and a plan for experimental implementation.

Instructions:

> 1. Define Instructional Improvement Goals:
>
>> ○ Identify specific goals or areas in your teaching practice where you seek

innovation or improvement.

2. Craft AI Discovery Prompts:

   ○ Write AI prompts such as "Identify innovative teaching methods recently applied in [subject area] for [target age group] that promote active learning and student engagement."

3. Gather AI-Generated Teaching Strategies:

   ○ Use the AI tool with your prompts to discover new and innovative teaching methods. Select those that align with your goals and educational context.

4. Develop an Implementation Plan:

   ○ Choose one or two new teaching methods to try. Develop a detailed plan for integrating these methods into an upcoming lesson or unit, considering materials, student activities, and assessment strategies.

5. Evaluate and Reflect on the Implementation:

   ○ After implementing the new methods, evaluate their effectiveness based on student feedback and learning outcomes. Reflect on the experience and consider further adaptations or continued use.

Activity 3: Integrating Technology Trends into the Curriculum

Tools & Materials Needed:

- AI technology trend analysis tool

- Current curriculum documents

- Checklist for evaluating educational technology integration

Time Needed: 3-4 hours

Outcome: A revised curriculum section that incorporates current technology trends relevant to your teaching area.

Instructions:

1. Identify Relevant Tech Trends:

   ○ Pinpoint areas within your curriculum where integrating new technology trends could enhance learning outcomes and student engagement.

2. Formulate AI Technology Trend Prompts:

- ○ Develop AI prompts like "Provide a list of current technology trends relevant to teaching [specific subject or skill] and suggest practical applications for middle school students."

3. Execute AI Trend Analysis:

- ○ Use the AI tool to identify relevant technology trends and applications. Review the AI-generated suggestions for appropriateness and feasibility.

4. Revise Curriculum with Tech Integrations:

- ○ Select suitable technology applications from the AI suggestions. Revise a section of your curriculum to include these technology integrations, outlining objectives, activities, and expected outcomes.

5. Implement and Review:

- ○ Implement the revised curriculum section in your classroom. Afterwards, review the impact on student engagement and learning, adjusting as necessary based on feedback and observations.

6. Post-Implementation AI Prompt for Educators:

- ○ "Generate a reflection guide to assess the effectiveness of integrating [specified technology trends] into the curriculum, focusing on student responses, engagement, and achievement."

By engaging in these activities, educators can leverage AI to stay updated with the latest trends and research in education, continuously enhancing their teaching methods and curriculum with fresh, relevant content. This ongoing professional development supports a dynamic learning environment where both teachers and students can thrive.

7.4 Integrating New Technologies into Teaching

In today's rapidly evolving educational landscape, the integration of new technologies into teaching practices is essential for creating dynamic and engaging learning environments. These technologies can offer innovative ways to deliver content, facilitate collaboration, and assess student understanding, thereby enhancing the overall educational experience. However, the effectiveness of these tools hinges on educators' proficiency and comfort with them. As such, continuous professional development in educational technology is crucial for teachers to stay current and make informed decisions about integrating these tools into their classrooms.

Custom AI prompts can serve as a valuable resource for educators looking to expand their technological toolkit. By leveraging AI, educators can discover the latest educational technologies tailored to their specific teaching needs and subject areas. These AI-generated recommendations can introduce teachers to a wide range of tools, from interactive whiteboards and educational apps to virtual reality experiences and online collaborative platforms. This approach ensures that educators are exposed to the most relevant and impactful technologies available.

The integration of new technologies into teaching not only supports student learning but also encourages teachers to experiment with and adopt innovative instructional strategies. It promotes a culture of lifelong learning among educators, encouraging them to continually refine their practices and explore new possibilities in the digital age. By remaining open to technological advancements, educators can provide their students with a richer, more varied educational experience that prepares them for the future.

Activity 1: Exploring and Implementing an Interactive Learning Platform

Tools & Materials Needed:

- Access to an AI tool for educational technology recommendations

- Digital device and internet connection

- Evaluation form for assessing technology effectiveness

Time Needed: 2-3 class periods

Outcome: Successful integration of a new interactive learning platform into the classroom and evaluated impact on student engagement.

Instructions:

1. Identify Educational Needs:

    ○ Assess your current teaching practices and identify areas where a new technology could enhance learning outcomes, such as student engagement or differentiated instruction.

2. Generate AI Technology Discovery Prompts:

    ○ Formulate AI prompts like "Identify interactive learning platforms suitable for enhancing student engagement in high school biology."

3. Research and Select a Technology Tool:

    ○ Use the AI-generated suggestions to research and select an interactive learning platform that aligns with your educational needs and objectives.

4. Plan and Implement the Tool:

    ○ Develop a lesson plan incorporating the chosen technology. Prepare any necessary materials and ensure you are comfortable using the platform before introducing it to students.

5. Evaluate and Reflect:

- ○ After implementing the technology in the classroom, use the evaluation form to assess its impact on student engagement and learning outcomes. Gather student feedback to inform further use and integration.

Activity 2: Integrating a New Assessment Tool

Tools & Materials Needed:

- AI tool for discovering educational technologies

- Access to the chosen new assessment tool

- Guidelines for effective assessment

Time Needed: 1-2 class periods

Outcome: Integration of a novel assessment tool into teaching practice and assessment of its effectiveness in providing meaningful feedback.

Instructions:

1. Determine Assessment Requirements:

- ○ Reflect on your current assessment strategies and identify potential improvements or gaps that a new technology could address.

2. Craft AI Assessment Tool Prompts:

- ○ Create AI prompts such as "Recommend innovative assessment tools for evaluating student understanding in middle school math."

3. Select and Familiarize with the Tool:

- ○ Based on AI recommendations, choose a new assessment tool. Spend time familiarizing yourself with its features and functionalities.

4. Design and Conduct an Assessment:

- ○ Incorporate the new tool into an upcoming assessment activity. Design the assessment to make full use of the tool's capabilities and align with your learning objectives.

5. Analyze Tool Effectiveness:

- ○ Evaluate the effectiveness of the new assessment tool based on student performance and feedback. Consider the tool's impact on your ability to gauge student understanding and provide feedback.

Activity 3: Adopting a Collaborative Technology for Project-Based Learning

Tools & Materials Needed:

- AI recommendation system for educational technologies

- Criteria for selecting collaborative tools

- Project guidelines for students

Time Needed: 3-4 class periods

Outcome: Effective implementation of a new collaborative technology to support project-based learning and evaluation of its impact.

Instructions:

1. Identify Collaboration Needs:

    ○ Pinpoint the needs of your students regarding collaboration, particularly in the context of project-based learning.

2. Generate AI Collaboration Tool Prompts:

    ○ Develop AI prompts such as "Find the best collaborative technologies to facilitate project-based learning in a fifth-grade classroom."

3. Research and Choose a Collaborative Tool:

    ○ Use the AI tool to find and select a collaborative technology that meets the needs identified. Ensure the tool promotes effective communication and teamwork among students.

4. Plan and Implement a Collaborative Project:

    ○ Design a project that leverages the selected technology, clearly outlining the collaboration expectations and goals. Introduce the technology to students and guide them in its use throughout the project.

5. Assess and Reflect on the Collaboration:

    ○ After the project's completion, assess the effectiveness of the collaborative technology in enhancing teamwork and learning outcomes. Collect student feedback to determine the tool's impact and areas for improvement.

6. Post-Implementation AI Prompt for Educators:

    ○ "Generate reflection questions to evaluate the integration and effectiveness of [selected technology] in enhancing collaborative project-based learning in my classroom."

Through these activities, educators not only expand their technological proficiency but also enrich their teaching methods, thereby enhancing student learning experiences and outcomes. The thoughtful selection and integration of new technologies, guided by AI, can lead to more engaged and effective learning environments.

7.5 Evaluating and Reflecting on Professional Development Activities

Professional development is an ongoing journey for educators, aimed at enhancing their skills and effectiveness in fostering student learning. Evaluating the impact of professional development activities is crucial to understand their effectiveness and to guide future learning opportunities. This evaluation process helps educators to reflect on what they have learned, how they have applied it, and the effect it has had on their teaching practices and student outcomes. Proper assessment can illuminate areas of success as well as areas needing further improvement or exploration.

Incorporating AI into this reflective process can significantly enhance the depth and breadth of evaluation. Feedback-oriented AI prompts can guide educators through a comprehensive self-reflection on their professional development experiences, prompting them to consider various aspects of their learning and its application. By utilizing AI, educators can receive personalized, targeted questions that prompt deeper reflection and generate constructive feedback forms tailored to their specific professional development activities.

The ultimate goal of this evaluative process is to ensure that professional development activities are not just completed but are effectively contributing to teaching excellence and student success. Through structured reflection guided by AI, educators can gain more nuanced insights into their professional growth, leading to more informed decisions about their ongoing educational journey and the selection of future professional development opportunities.

Activity 1: Reflective Analysis of a Professional Development Workshop

Tools & Materials Needed:

- AI tool capable of generating reflective evaluation prompts

- Access to personal notes and materials from the professional development workshop

- Template for recording reflections and action plans

Time Needed: 1-2 hours

Outcome: A detailed reflective analysis of the professional development workshop and a clear action plan for applying learned concepts in the classroom.

Instructions:

1. Prepare Your Reflection Materials:

   ○ Gather any notes, resources, or materials from the recent professional development workshop you attended.

2. Generate AI Reflective Prompts:

   ○ Formulate AI prompts such as "Generate reflective questions to assess the application and impact of strategies learned during the [specific workshop] on my teaching practices and student engagement."

3. Conduct the Reflective Analysis:

   ○ Use the AI-generated prompts to guide your reflective analysis. Write down your responses, focusing on what you learned, how you have applied (or plan to apply) the strategies, and the observed or anticipated effects on your teaching and your students.

4. Develop an Action Plan:

   ○ Based on your reflections, outline a clear action plan for further integrating the workshop concepts into your teaching. Include specific steps, resources needed, and timelines.

5. Plan for Follow-up and Adjustment:

   ○ Determine how you will monitor the effectiveness of the implemented strategies. Plan for periodic reviews and adjustments based on student feedback and learning outcomes.

Activity 2: Evaluating a New Teaching Strategy Implementation

Tools & Materials Needed:

- AI tool for generating feedback and evaluation prompts

- Documentation of the new teaching strategy implementation (lesson plans, student work, assessments)

- Feedback form for student and peer input

Time Needed: 2 hours

Outcome: A comprehensive evaluation of a newly implemented teaching strategy, incorporating personal reflection, student feedback, and peer observations.

Instructions:

1. Document the Implementation Process:

   ○ Record details of how you implemented the new teaching strategy, including planning, execution, student reactions, and any observed outcomes.

2. Generate AI Evaluation Prompts:

   ○ Create AI prompts such as "Develop a set of questions for evaluating the effectiveness and impact of [specific teaching strategy] on student learning and engagement."

3. Perform the Evaluation:

   ○ Use the AI-generated prompts to guide your evaluation of the teaching strategy. Reflect on your experiences, gather student feedback using the prepared forms, and incorporate any peer observations.

4. Analyze Feedback and Outcomes:

   ○ Review all collected data and feedback to assess the success of the teaching strategy. Identify strengths, challenges, and any noticeable impacts on student engagement and learning.

5. Outline Improvements and Next Steps:

   ○ Based on the evaluation, note areas for improvement and plan any necessary adjustments to the teaching strategy. Consider additional professional development needs or resources to enhance future implementations.

Activity 3: Post-Professional Development Project Review

Tools & Materials Needed:

- AI tool for post-project reflection and evaluation

- Completed professional development project or initiative documentation

- Evaluation metrics or criteria aligned with project goals

Time Needed: 3-4 hours

Outcome: Detailed project review highlighting successes, challenges, and lessons learned for future professional development planning.

Instructions:

1. Prepare Project Documentation:

   ○ Collect all relevant documentation, outcomes, and feedback related to your professional development project or initiative.

2. Formulate AI Post-Project Prompts:

   ○ Develop AI prompts such as "Analyze the outcomes of [specific project] against the initial professional development goals and provide a comprehensive review."

3. Conduct the Project Review:

   ○ Use the responses generated by the AI to evaluate the overall success and impact of your professional development project. Consider aspects such as knowledge gained, skills applied, student reactions, and any changes in teaching efficacy.

4. Compile Lessons Learned and Successes:

   ○ Document key takeaways, successful elements, and areas where expectations were not met. Reflect on the reasons behind these outcomes and what could be done differently in the future.

5. Develop Future Professional Development Plans:

   ○ Based on the review, identify new areas for professional growth and outline plans for future professional development activities. Include specific goals, needed resources, and potential challenges.

6. Post-Implementation AI Prompt for Educators:

   ○ "Generate follow-up questions to guide continuous reflection and growth following the completion of a professional development project, focusing on long-term integration of learned strategies and sustained improvement in teaching practices."

These activities, underpinned by thoughtful AI-generated prompts, enable educators to systematically evaluate and reflect on their professional development efforts, leading to more targeted and effective future growth initiatives.

Chapter Eight

Prompts for Administrative Tasks

8.1 Streamlining Scheduling and Planning

Efficient scheduling and planning are critical components in the educational environment, enabling schools to maximize instructional time, effectively utilize resources, and maintain a well-ordered educational atmosphere. The challenge of juggling multiple schedules, including classes, teacher assignments, and room allocations, can be daunting. However, with the integration of AI technology, these tasks can become more streamlined and less time-consuming, allowing educators and administrators to focus more on teaching and less on administrative tasks.

AI prompts can be specifically designed to assist in the organization of school schedules, teacher assignments, and room allocations. By leveraging AI, schools can optimize their scheduling processes, ensuring that resources are used efficiently and that all students have access to the courses and educators they need. AI can analyze vast amounts of data to identify the most effective scheduling patterns, suggest optimal room usage, and balance teacher workloads, all while considering the unique needs and constraints of the school.

The implementation of AI in scheduling and planning not only increases efficiency but also improves overall school operations. By automating complex and time-consuming tasks, AI enables administrators to quickly respond to changes and make data-driven decisions that benefit both teachers and students. By guiding educators or administrators in using AI for these tasks, they can experience firsthand the benefits of technology-enhanced management in the educational setting.

Activity 1: Creating an AI-Enhanced School Event Calendar

Tools & Materials Needed:

- AI scheduling tool with calendar integration

- List of school events, holidays, and important dates

- Criteria for event scheduling (e.g., grade levels involved, space requirements)

Time Needed: 2 hours

Outcome: A comprehensive school event calendar optimized by AI, facilitating the efficient organization of school-wide activities.

Instructions:

1. Compile School Events Information:

    ○ Gather all necessary information regarding upcoming school events, including dates, participating grades, and space needs.

2. Generate AI Scheduling Prompts:

    ○ Develop AI prompts such as "Organize these school events into an annual calendar, avoiding conflicts and considering optimal times for student participation and facility availability."

3. Input Data into AI Scheduling Tool:

    ○ Enter the list of events and AI prompts into the scheduling tool. Let the AI process the information and generate a preliminary event calendar.

4. Review and Adjust the AI-Generated Calendar:

    ○ Examine the AI-suggested calendar, making adjustments as necessary to accommodate school-specific needs and preferences that the AI might not have considered.

5. Evaluate and Finalize the Calendar:

    ○ Assess the effectiveness of the AI-generated calendar in streamlining event planning and addressing the school's requirements. Finalize the calendar for distribution to staff, students, and parents.

Activity 2: Developing a Teacher Duty Roster with AI Assistance

Tools & Materials Needed:

- AI tool for roster creation

- List of teacher names, subjects taught, and available times

- School policies on teacher duties and workload balance

Time Needed: 3 hours

Outcome: An equitable and well-organized teacher duty roster created with the help of AI, promoting balanced workloads and efficient resource use.

Instructions:

1. Assemble Teacher Availability Data:

   - Collect information on each teacher's availability, subjects, and current workload.

2. Craft AI Roster Creation Prompts:

   - Write AI prompts such as "Generate a balanced duty roster for teachers based on their available times, workload, and subject specialties, ensuring fair distribution of duties."

3. Utilize the AI Tool for Roster Development:

   - Input the teacher data and AI prompts into the tool. Analyze the AI-suggested duty roster, noting how duties are allocated among staff.

4. Adjust and Optimize the Roster:

   - Make necessary adjustments to the AI-generated roster to address any overlooked individual needs or school-specific considerations.

5. Implement, Monitor, and Gather Feedback:

   - Roll out the new duty roster, monitor its implementation, and collect feedback from teachers regarding its fairness and effectiveness.

Activity 3: AI-Optimized Room Allocation for Classes and Events

Tools & Materials Needed:

- AI room allocation software

- Classroom and event space specifications

- Class sizes, special needs, and equipment requirements

Time Needed: 4 hours

Outcome: An optimized room allocation plan for classes and events, enhancing the utilization of school spaces.

Instructions:

1. Detail Room and Class Requirements:

- ○ List all available rooms and their features alongside the requirements for each class and event, including size, special equipment, and accessibility.

2. Generate AI Allocation Prompts:

- ○ Create AI prompts like "Allocate rooms for the upcoming semester's classes and events, considering class size, special needs, and equipment requirements, while maximizing space utilization."

3. Engage the AI Room Allocation Tool:

- ○ Enter the detailed requirements and AI prompts into the software. Review the AI's room allocation suggestions for efficiency and suitability.

4. Review and Adjust Allocations:

- ○ Check the AI-assisted allocation plan against known constraints and preferences. Adjust as needed to ensure the best fit for all classes and events.

5. Evaluate Effectiveness and Collect Feedback:

- ○ After implementing the AI-optimized room plan, evaluate its effectiveness in meeting the needs of teachers and students. Collect feedback to inform future allocations.

6. Post-Implementation AI Prompt for Educators/Administrators:

- ○ "Generate a survey to assess teacher and student satisfaction with the new scheduling and room allocations, focusing on areas for improvement and suggestions for future planning."

These activities facilitate the practical application of AI in streamlining school scheduling and planning tasks, demonstrating the significant advantages of integrating technology into educational administration.

8.2 Enhancing Reporting and Record-Keeping

Accurate reporting and diligent record-keeping are indispensable in the educational sector for tracking student progress, understanding institutional performance, and making informed decisions. These tasks, while crucial, can often be time-consuming and prone to human error. The advent of AI technologies offers a promising solution, automating the compilation, analysis, and presentation of educational data, thereby enhancing the accuracy and efficiency of reporting processes.

By employing interactive AI prompts, educators and administrators can streamline the creation of various reports, from attendance records and grade distributions to budget expenditures and resource utilization. AI can assist in identifying trends, anomalies, and areas needing attention, transforming raw data into actionable insights. This not only saves valuable time but also allows for a deeper analysis of the data, contributing to a more nuanced understanding of student achievements and institutional challenges.

Integrating AI into reporting and record-keeping processes fosters a culture of transparency and accountability within educational institutions. It enables educators to provide stakeholders with precise and timely information, enhancing communication and collaboration between schools, families, and communities. Furthermore, AI-generated reports can support continuous improvement by highlighting successes and pinpointing areas for development, thereby contributing to the overall effectiveness and quality of education.

Activity 1: AI-Generated Attendance and Participation Report

Tools & Materials Needed:

- AI-powered data analysis tool

- School attendance records

- Guidelines for interpreting attendance data

Time Needed: 2 hours

Outcome: A comprehensive AI-generated report on student attendance and participation, identifying patterns and areas for improvement.

Instructions:

1. Collect Attendance Records:

    ○ Gather recent attendance records for a specified period. Ensure the data is complete and accurately reflects student attendance.

2. Develop AI Reporting Prompts:

    ○ Formulate AI prompts such as "Analyze the attendance records for the past semester, identify trends and correlations with student performance, and suggest interventions for improving attendance rates."

3. Create the Attendance Report:

    ○ Input the attendance data and AI prompts into the data analysis tool. Review the AI-generated report, focusing on identified trends, anomalies, and suggested interventions.

4. Evaluate Report Findings:

    ○ Assess the clarity and comprehensiveness of the AI-generated report. Determine the practicality of the suggested interventions and plan for their implementation.

5. Share and Discuss the Report:

   ○ Share the report with relevant stakeholders (e.g., teaching staff, student counselors) and discuss actionable steps to address attendance issues.

Activity 2: Analyzing Grade Distributions with AI

Tools & Materials Needed:

- AI analysis software

- Grade distribution data for different classes or subjects

- Criteria for evaluating academic performance

Time Needed: 3 hours

Outcome: An insightful AI-generated report on grade distributions, highlighting academic strengths and areas needing attention.

Instructions:

1. Gather Grade Data:

   ○ Compile grade distribution data from recent assessments across various classes or subjects.

2. Generate AI Analysis Prompts:

   ○ Write AI prompts like "Generate a report analyzing the grade distributions for [specific classes/subjects], highlighting patterns, outliers, and potential underlying causes."

3. Produce the Grade Distribution Report:

   ○ Use the AI software to analyze the grade data based on your prompts. Examine the resulting report for insights into student achievements and challenges.

4. Interpret and Reflect on Findings:

   ○ Review the AI-generated insights, identifying areas where students excel and where additional support may be needed.

5. Plan for Academic Interventions:

   ○ Based on the report, strategize academic interventions or enrichment programs. Consider scheduling meetings with teaching teams to discuss and implement these plans.

Activity 3: AI-Assisted Budget Expenditure Review

Tools & Materials Needed:

- Financial data analysis tool with AI capabilities

- School budget and expenditure records for the current or previous fiscal year

- Guidelines for budget analysis and financial planning

Time Needed: 4 hours

Outcome: A detailed AI-generated report on school budget expenditures, assessing financial efficiency and identifying cost-saving opportunities.

Instructions:

1. Compile Financial Data:

    ○ Organize comprehensive budget and expenditure records for analysis.

2. Formulate AI Financial Review Prompts:

    ○ Develop AI prompts such as "Review the school's budget expenditures for the fiscal year, compare actual spending against the budget, and identify areas for financial optimization."

3. Conduct the Financial Analysis:

    ○ Input the financial data and AI prompts into the analysis tool. Review the generated financial report, focusing on spending trends, budget adherence, and recommendations for cost savings.

4. Assess and Plan Based on the Report:

    ○ Evaluate the AI report's findings, considering their implications for future budget planning and resource allocation.

5. Discuss and Implement Recommendations:

    ○ Share the report with school financial planners and administrative staff. Discuss feasible recommendations and plan their implementation to improve financial efficiency.

6. Post-Implementation AI Prompt for Educators/Administrators:

    ○ "Generate a follow-up survey to evaluate the effectiveness and impact of changes made based on the AI-generated reports in improving school operations, student attendance, academic performance, and financial management."

These activities enable educators and administrators to leverage AI in enhancing the efficiency and accuracy of school reporting and record-keeping processes, ultimately facilitating better-informed decision-making and improving educational outcomes.

8.3 Improving Communication with Stakeholders

Effective communication with stakeholders, including parents, students, and community members, is crucial in the educational landscape. It ensures that everyone involved is informed, engaged, and working towards common goals. Clear and consistent outreach helps in building trust, fostering a sense of community, and ensuring the success of students. However, crafting messages that are informative, engaging, and clear can be challenging, especially when addressing diverse audiences with varying needs and expectations.

Incorporating AI into the communication process can significantly enhance the quality and effectiveness of outreach efforts. AI prompts can assist educators in generating well-structured, relevant, and audience-tailored content for newsletters, announcements, parent letters, and more. By leveraging AI, educators can ensure that their communications are not only informative but also engaging and accessible, thereby improving the likelihood of positive stakeholder response and involvement.

Using AI-generated drafts as a starting point, educators can save time while maintaining a high standard of communication. The AI can suggest content based on recent school activities, upcoming events, policy changes, or educational tips, which educators can then personalize to reflect the school's tone and values. This approach ensures that all stakeholders remain well-informed and connected to the school's educational journey, fostering a collaborative and supportive environment.

Activity 1: Crafting an AI-Generated Newsletter for Parents

Tools & Materials Needed:

- AI text generation tool

- Information on recent school activities and upcoming events

- Guidelines for school communication tone and style

Time Needed: 1-2 hours

Outcome: A well-crafted, AI-generated newsletter ready to be shared with parents, fostering improved school-family communication.

Instructions:

1. Gather Content Information:

- Compile details on recent school achievements, upcoming events, and important announcements.

2. Generate AI Communication Prompts:

- Develop AI prompts like "Create a newsletter draft for parents highlighting recent school achievements, upcoming events, and important policy updates, maintaining a positive and engaging tone."

3. Create the Newsletter Draft:

- Use the AI tool with your prompts to generate a draft of the newsletter. Review the AI-generated content, ensuring it aligns with the provided information and adheres to the school's communication standards.

4. Personalize and Finalize the Newsletter:

- Personalize the AI-generated draft with specific details, quotes, or messages from the school staff. Ensure the final newsletter is clear, informative, and reflective of the school's values.

5. Distribute and Collect Feedback:

- Share the finalized newsletter with parents via email, the school's website, or printed copies. Later, collect feedback to assess the effectiveness of the communication and make improvements for future newsletters.

Activity 2: AI-Assisted Parent Letter on Policy Changes

Tools & Materials Needed:

- AI writing assistant

- Details on the specific policy changes

- School letterhead or email template

Time Needed: 1 hour

Outcome: A clear and comprehensive letter to parents, explaining recent policy changes and addressing potential concerns or questions.

Instructions:

1. Outline Policy Changes:

- Summarize the policy changes, including the reasons behind them and the expected impact on students and families.

2. Formulate AI Writing Prompts:

- Construct AI prompts such as "Generate a parent letter explaining the recent policy changes, including rationale, benefits, and answers to anticipated questions, while ensuring a supportive and understanding tone."

3. Generate and Review the Letter Draft:

- Input the prompts into the AI writing assistant to produce a draft letter. Carefully review and revise the AI-generated text to ensure accuracy, clarity, and empathy.

4. Personalize and Approve the Letter:

- Add personal touches to the letter, such as direct contacts for parents with further questions. Ensure the final version is respectful, informative, and aligned with school policies.

5. Send and Solicit Feedback:

- Distribute the letter to parents via the school's preferred communication channels. Follow up to solicit feedback and address any resulting concerns or questions.

Activity 3: Developing an Announcement for an Upcoming School Event

Tools & Materials Needed:

- AI content creation tool

- Details of the upcoming school event, including date, time, location, and purpose

- Instructions for response or participation

Time Needed: 1-2 hours

Outcome: An engaging and informative announcement for the upcoming school event, crafted to maximize attendance and participation.

Instructions:

1. Detail the Event:

- Collect all relevant information regarding the upcoming school event.

2. Generate AI Announcement Prompts:

- Create AI prompts such as "Write an engaging announcement for [specific event], detailing the purpose, date, time, and location, and encouraging parental involvement and student participation."

3. Produce and Refine the Announcement:

- Use the AI tool with the provided prompts to generate the event announcement. Review and refine the AI-generated content to ensure it is compelling, clear, and complete.

4. Personalize and Approve the Announcement:

- Personalize the announcement with any additional details, school-specific language, or calls to action. Confirm that the final version is ready for distribution.

5. Disseminate and Evaluate Response:

- Share the announcement through various school communication channels. Monitor the response to gauge effectiveness and gather insights for future communications.

6. Post-Implementation AI Prompt for Educators:

- "Generate a feedback form for stakeholders to evaluate the clarity, relevance, and engagement of the recent communications regarding the school event or policy change."

Through these activities, educators can utilize AI to enhance the clarity, efficiency, and engagement of their communications with stakeholders, ensuring that important information is effectively conveyed and fostering a stronger school community.

8.4 Managing Resources and Inventory

Effective resource and inventory management is a cornerstone of efficient educational operation, ensuring that valuable assets such as textbooks, technology, and various supplies are optimally utilized and accounted for. Proper management supports not only day-to-day educational activities but also aids in strategic budgeting and planning, reducing waste and ensuring that resources are available where and when they are needed most. In environments where resources are often limited, the ability to track, allocate, and forecast resource needs becomes essential for sustaining high-quality educational offerings.

Integrating AI into the process of managing resources and inventory can significantly enhance these efforts. Custom AI prompts can be designed to assist educators and administrators in accurately tracking resource usage, predicting future needs based on historical data, and identifying discrepancies or areas of surplus. This level of analysis and insight allows for more informed decision-making, ensuring that resources are allocated efficiently and effectively across the educational institution.

By leveraging AI for resource and inventory management, schools can achieve a greater level of operational excellence. The ability to swiftly identify areas of need or surplus not only optimizes resource utilization but also contributes to a more dynamic and responsive educational environment. Teachers and students alike benefit from having the right resources at the right time, enhancing the overall learning experience and supporting educational success.

Activity 1: AI-Assisted Textbook Inventory Audit

Tools & Materials Needed:

- AI tool capable of analyzing inventory data

- Current inventory records of textbooks and educational materials

- Access to historical usage and procurement data

Time Needed: 3-4 hours

Outcome: An accurate audit of textbook inventory, highlighting areas of surplus and need, facilitated by AI-generated analysis.

Instructions:

1. Compile Inventory Data:

   - Gather the most recent inventory records of textbooks and related educational materials, including quantities and conditions.

2. Generate AI Audit Prompts:

   - Develop AI prompts such as "Analyze the current textbook inventory against historical usage patterns and forecast future needs for each subject area."

3. Conduct the AI Inventory Audit:

   - Input your inventory data and AI prompts into the tool. Review the AI-generated report for insights into surplus areas and potential shortages.

4. Identify Action Items:

   - Based on the AI analysis, identify textbooks that are in surplus and those that may require replenishment or updating. Create a prioritized action list for addressing these findings.

5. Plan for Resource Reallocation or Procurement:

   - Develop a plan for reallocating surplus resources and procuring additional textbooks or materials as needed, based on the AI audit results.

Activity 2: Tracking Technology Assets with AI

Tools & Materials Needed:

- AI-based asset management software

- List of technology assets (e.g., laptops, tablets, projectors)

- Criteria for technology allocation and replacement

Time Needed: 2-3 hours

Outcome: A detailed review of the school's technology assets, with AI insights on allocation efficiency and replacement needs.

Instructions:

1. List Technology Assets:

   ○ Document all technology assets currently in use or in storage, including model numbers, condition, and current allocation (if applicable).

2. Formulate AI Tracking Prompts:

   ○ Write AI prompts like "Evaluate the current allocation of technology assets to ensure optimal utilization and identify items due for replacement or maintenance."

3. Execute AI Asset Tracking:

   ○ Use the AI-based asset management software with your prompts to analyze the technology inventory. Pay attention to the AI's recommendations for reallocating underused assets or flagging those needing replacement.

4. Review AI Recommendations:

   ○ Assess the AI-generated advice on asset allocation and replacement. Determine the feasibility and priority of these recommendations.

5. Implement Changes and Monitor Results:

   ○ Adjust technology allocations according to the AI suggestions. Plan for the acquisition of new assets or the maintenance of existing ones as recommended. Monitor the impact of these changes on educational delivery.

Activity 3: AI-Powered Supply Needs Forecast

Tools & Materials Needed:

- AI forecasting tool

- Historical supply usage data (e.g., art supplies, lab materials)

- Upcoming curriculum plans and expected class sizes

Time Needed: 2-3 hours

Outcome: A forecast of classroom supply needs, utilizing AI to predict future requirements based on historical data and upcoming educational activities.

Instructions:

1. Gather Historical Usage Data:

   ○ Compile data on past usage of various classroom supplies, considering seasonal or curriculum-related fluctuations.

2. Develop AI Forecasting Prompts:

   ○ Create AI prompts like "Predict the classroom supply needs for the upcoming semester, considering historical usage patterns and the expected number of students."

3. Perform AI-Powered Forecasting:

   ○ Input the historical data and upcoming plans into the AI forecasting tool. Review the predictions for supply needs, focusing on accuracy and practicality.

4. Identify Procurement Priorities:

   ○ Based on the AI forecast, identify supplies that require immediate procurement or restocking. Prioritize these based on upcoming curriculum needs and budget considerations.

5. Plan and Execute Procurement:

   ○ Develop a procurement plan addressing the identified needs. Implement the plan, ensuring that all necessary supplies are acquired in time for their intended use.

6. Post-Implementation AI Prompt for Educators/Administrators:

   ○ "Generate a follow-up analysis to compare the AI-predicted supply needs against actual usage, identifying areas for improvement in future forecasting."

By engaging in these activities, educators and administrators can leverage AI to significantly improve the management of resources and inventory, leading to more efficient and effective educational environments.

8.5 Automating Routine Communications and Inquiries

In the bustling environment of educational institutions, managing routine communications and inquiries can consume a significant portion of the administrative and teaching staff's time. These routine interactions, while important, can detract from focusing on more pressing educational duties and responsibilities. Automating standard communications and common inquiries through AI can revolutionize how schools interact with their communities. By utilizing AI-driven systems, schools can ensure timely, accurate, and consistent responses, enhancing the overall communication experience for students, parents, and staff.

Implementing AI for routine communications allows for the automation of responses to frequently asked questions, the generation of standardized email replies, and the operation of chatbots on school websites. This not only reduces the administrative workload but also provides immediate assistance and information to stakeholders, improving satisfaction and trust in the school's operational efficiency. Feedback-oriented AI prompts can further refine these automated systems, tailoring interactions to meet the specific needs and queries of the school community while maintaining a personal touch.

The integration of AI-driven communication systems into school operations underscores a commitment to technological advancement and customer service excellence. By streamlining interactions and automating routine inquiries, educational institutions can allocate more resources to enhancing student learning experiences and supporting faculty needs. This shift not only optimizes administrative workflows but also fosters a more engaged and informed school community.

Activity 1: Developing an AI-Enabled FAQ Section for the School Website

Tools & Materials Needed:

- AI content generation tool

- List of frequently asked questions (FAQs) by students, parents, and community members

- Access to the school website's content management system

Time Needed: 2-3 hours

Outcome: An AI-generated FAQ section on the school website, providing instant, accurate information to common inquiries.

Instructions:

1. Compile Common Inquiries:

- Gather a comprehensive list of frequently asked questions from students, parents, and other stakeholders.

2. Create AI Generation Prompts:

- Develop AI prompts such as "Generate concise, informative responses for the following common school-related inquiries, maintaining a friendly and professional tone."

3. Generate FAQ Content:

- Use the AI content generation tool with your prompts to create responses for each FAQ. Ensure that the answers are accurate, clear, and reflect the school's policies and values.

4. Implement the FAQ Section:

- Upload the AI-generated FAQ content to the school website's FAQ section. Organize the questions and answers for easy navigation and user-friendliness.

5. Monitor and Evaluate:

- Track the usage and feedback on the new FAQ section. Assess whether inquiries have decreased and evaluate user satisfaction to identify areas for improvement.

Activity 2: Setting Up an AI-Driven Email Response System

Tools & Materials Needed:

- AI-driven email management software

- Templates for common types of school-related inquiries

- Training guide for using the AI email system

Time Needed: 4 hours

Outcome: An automated email response system that efficiently handles routine school inquiries.

Instructions:

1. Identify Email Inquiry Categories:

- Determine the most common types of inquiries received via the school's email system (e.g., admission queries, event information).

2. Generate AI Email Templates:

○ Formulate AI prompts such as "Create email response templates for the following inquiry categories, ensuring clarity, warmth, and alignment with school guidelines."

3. Set Up the AI Email System:

○ Implement the AI-driven email management software, integrating the AI-generated response templates. Configure the system to categorize and respond to common inquiries automatically.

4. Train Staff and Launch the System:

○ Train relevant staff on the new system, providing guidelines for monitoring and intervening when necessary. Officially launch the automated response system.

5. Review and Optimize:

○ Regularly review the system's performance, analyzing response times, accuracy, and user satisfaction. Make adjustments based on feedback and evolving communication needs.

Activity 3: Implementing an AI Chatbot for the School Website

Tools & Materials Needed:

- AI chatbot development platform

- List of scenarios and questions for the chatbot to handle

- Integration guide for the school website

Time Needed: 3-4 hours

Outcome: A functional AI chatbot on the school website, providing real-time answers to visitors' questions.

Instructions:

1. Outline Chatbot Capabilities:

○ Define the range of questions and scenarios the chatbot should be able to handle, based on common stakeholder inquiries.

2. Develop AI Chatbot Prompts:

○ Craft AI prompts like "Design chatbot dialogues for handling typical inquiries about school hours, enrollment procedures, and upcoming events."

3. Create and Train the Chatbot:

- Use the AI chatbot development platform to create the chatbot based on the prompts. Train the chatbot using the defined scenarios to ensure accurate and helpful responses.

4. Integrate the Chatbot into the School Website:

- Follow the integration guide to add the chatbot to the school website, ensuring it is easily accessible and user-friendly.

5. Monitor, Gather Feedback, and Refine:

- Monitor the chatbot's interactions, collecting user feedback to assess satisfaction and effectiveness. Refine the chatbot's responses and capabilities based on this feedback to improve user experience.

6. Post-Implementation AI Prompt for Educators/Administrators:

- "Generate a survey to collect feedback from students, parents, and teachers on their experiences with the new AI communication tools, focusing on areas of success and suggestions for enhancements."

These activities enable educators and administrators to harness AI technology to automate routine communications, improving efficiency and stakeholder satisfaction while allowing staff to dedicate more time to pressing educational needs.

Chapter Nine

Building Your AI Toolkit

9.1 Understanding AI Capabilities and Limitations

The integration of Artificial Intelligence (AI) into educational settings is rapidly expanding, offering new opportunities for enhancing teaching and learning processes. However, with the adoption of any new technology, it is essential to understand not only its capabilities but also its limitations. This foundational knowledge is crucial for setting realistic expectations for AI integration in educational settings. By understanding what AI can and cannot do, educators can make informed decisions about how to effectively incorporate AI tools into their teaching strategies and administrative tasks.

AI literacy among educators is becoming increasingly important as AI technologies become more prevalent in educational environments. Educators need to understand different types of AI, how they operate, and their potential applications within educational settings. This includes knowledge of data-driven decision-making processes, natural language processing, machine learning models, and ethical considerations. By becoming AI-literate, educators can better evaluate AI tools and platforms, ensuring they align with educational goals and student needs while addressing concerns such as data privacy and algorithmic bias.

To foster AI literacy, educators should engage in ongoing professional development that includes exploring AI's current uses in education, potential future applications, and critical discussions about ethical implications. By building a comprehensive understanding of AI, educators can more effectively integrate AI solutions that enhance learning outcomes, streamline administrative tasks, and prepare students for a future in which AI plays an increasingly significant role.

Activity 1: AI Literacy Self-Assessment and Learning Path Enhancement

Tools & Materials Needed:

- AI literacy self-assessment tool or questionnaire

- Access to a range of AI educational resources (online courses, articles, tutorials)

- Personalized learning path template

Time Needed: 3 hours

Outcome: A completed AI literacy self-assessment and a personalized learning path to enhance AI understanding and application in educational settings.

Instructions:

1. Conduct an AI Literacy Self-Assessment:

   ○ Utilize the AI literacy self-assessment tool to evaluate current levels of understanding regarding AI's capabilities, types, and educational applications.

2. Develop AI Learning Objectives:

   ○ Based on the self-assessment outcomes, craft AI prompts such as "Identify areas of AI literacy needing improvement and suggest targeted educational resources."

3. Outline a Personalized Learning Path:

   ○ Employ the learning path template to map out a strategy for addressing knowledge gaps, utilizing AI prompts like "Create a structured learning path based on identified AI literacy gaps."

4. Engage with Selected AI Educational Resources:

   ○ Begin working through the selected resources, applying AI prompts such as "Summarize key takeaways from [specific resource] and how they can be applied in an educational context."

5. Reflect and Share Insights:

   ○ Reflect on the learning journey using prompts like "Evaluate the impact of the completed learning path on my AI literacy and instructional practice." Share outcomes and insights with peers for collaborative learning and feedback.

6. Post-Implementation AI Prompt for Educators:

   ○ "Construct a reflective questionnaire to assess ongoing AI literacy development and identify future learning goals."

Activity 2: Customizing AI for Classroom Management

Tools & Materials Needed:

- Access to AI-powered classroom management software

- List of common classroom management challenges

- AI prompt refinement guide

Time Needed: 4 hours

Outcome: Customized AI solutions tailored to address specific classroom management challenges.

Instructions:

1. Identify Classroom Management Challenges:

   ○ List typical classroom management challenges that could be addressed with AI support.

2. Generate AI Solution Prompts:

   ○ Create specific AI prompts such as "Generate classroom management strategies for improving student engagement based on AI analysis."

3. Implement AI-driven Strategies:

   ○ Apply the created AI prompts within the classroom management software, tailoring the AI's functionalities to meet the identified challenges.

4. Assess and Adapt AI Strategies:

   ○ Evaluate the effectiveness of AI-driven management strategies using prompts like "Assess the impact of applied AI strategies on classroom dynamics and student behavior."

5. Share Experiences and Optimize:

   ○ Share the developed AI strategies and outcomes with colleagues, using prompts for constructive feedback like "Provide insights on enhancing AI-driven classroom management tactics."

6. Post-Implementation AI Prompt for Educators:

   ○ "Devise a feedback collection mechanism to monitor the ongoing effectiveness of AI-driven classroom management solutions and identify areas for improvement."

Activity 3: Integrating AI Tools for Enhancing Educational Content

Tools & Materials Needed:

- Selection of AI tools relevant to content creation (e.g., content summarizers, question generators)

- Criteria for evaluating educational content enhancement

- Feedback and evaluation forms for content effectiveness

Time Needed: 3 hours

Outcome: Enhanced educational content through the integration of AI tools, with evaluated effectiveness based on student feedback and learning outcomes.

Instructions:

1. Select AI Content Enhancement Tools:

   - Choose AI tools that could enhance educational content delivery and engagement.

2. Develop Content Enhancement AI Prompts:

   - Craft AI prompts like "Enhance the educational content of [specific subject or topic] to increase student engagement and comprehension."

3. Apply and Integrate AI-Enhanced Content:

   - Implement the AI-generated content into lesson plans or educational materials, using scenarios and questions tailored to student needs.

4. Evaluate Content Effectiveness:

   - Collect student feedback on AI-enhanced content using structured evaluation forms, applying prompts like "Evaluate the student engagement level and understanding after introducing AI-enhanced content."

5. Revise and Improve AI-Integrated Content:

   - Based on feedback, refine the AI-enhanced educational content, employing prompts like "Modify the AI-enhanced content for [subject/topic] to better address student learning gaps."

6. Post-Implementation AI Prompt for Educators/Administrators:

   - "Create an analysis template to compare student performance and engagement before and after the implementation of AI-enhanced educational content."

9.2 Evaluating and Selecting AI Tools

Selecting the right AI tools for educational purposes is a nuanced process that demands thorough evaluation and understanding. The integration of AI into educational settings offers the potential to enhance learning experiences, streamline administrative tasks, and provide insights into student performance and engagement. However, to truly reap these benefits, educators and administrators must carefully assess the suitability of AI tools against a set of well-defined criteria. These criteria typically include the effectiveness of the tool in achieving educational objectives, its ease of use for both teachers and students, compatibility with existing educational systems and technologies, and adherence to privacy and data protection standards.

Moreover, the decision-making process for selecting AI tools should be structured and collaborative, involving stakeholders such as IT specialists, teachers, students, and parents where appropriate. This collaborative approach ensures that the selected AI tools align with the specific needs, goals, and constraints of the educational institution. Additionally, it is crucial to consider the ethical implications of AI tools, including potential biases and their impact on student equity and inclusivity. By following a comprehensive evaluation and selection process, educators can make informed decisions that positively impact student learning and operational efficiency.

Ultimately, the goal of evaluating and selecting AI tools is to find solutions that are not only technologically advanced but also pedagogically sound and ethically responsible. Educators need to stay informed about the latest AI developments, understand the capabilities and limitations of different AI tools, and consider the long-term implications of their integration into educational practices. By doing so, they can ensure that the adoption of AI technologies contributes to a more effective, engaging, and inclusive educational environment.

Certainly, incorporating AI-generated prompts into the instruction section can provide a clearer guide for participants undertaking these activities. Here's how the activities could be restructured to include specific AI generation prompts:

Activity 1: AI Tool Evaluation Workshop

Tools & Materials Needed:

- List of AI tools for evaluation

- Evaluation criteria checklist

- Evaluation forms or digital platform for recording assessments

- Case studies or demos of AI tools

Time Needed: 4 hours

Outcome: A comprehensive evaluation of several AI tools, leading to the selection of one tool for classroom or administrative pilot implementation.

Instructions:

1. Introduce AI Tools and Evaluation Criteria:

   ○ Distribute the evaluation criteria checklist and a list of AI tools. Provide an AI prompt example: "Evaluate [AI Tool Name] for its application in enhancing [specific educational outcome]."

2. Review and Assess AI Tools:

   ○ "Identify the key functionalities of [Assigned AI Tool] that align with our educational objectives and evaluate its user friendliness and integration capabilities."

3. Complete Evaluation Forms:

   ○ "Summarize the advantages and limitations of [Assigned AI Tool] based on our predefined criteria and suggest potential educational applications."

4. Present and Discuss Evaluations:

   ○ "Develop a presentation that outlines your group's findings on [Assigned AI Tool], highlighting its feasibility for our educational context."

5. Select AI Tool for Pilot Implementation:

   ○ "Based on our group discussions, recommend one AI tool for pilot implementation and justify your choice with specific evaluation points."

Activity 2: Developing AI Tool Implementation Plans

Tools & Materials Needed:

- Selected AI tool for pilot implementation

- Implementation plan template

- Feedback and evaluation mechanisms

Time Needed: 3 hours

Outcome: A detailed implementation plan for piloting the selected AI tool, including objectives, timelines, success metrics, and feedback mechanisms.

Instructions:

1. Outline Pilot Objectives and Scope:

    ○ "Define clear objectives for the implementation of [Selected AI Tool] within our educational setting and identify the scope of its application."

2. Define Implementation Steps:

    ○ "List the necessary steps for [Selected AI Tool] integration, including technical requirements and educational adjustments."

3. Establish Success Metrics and Evaluation Methods:

    ○ "Formulate success metrics for evaluating the impact of [Selected AI Tool] on student learning outcomes and engagement."

4. Prepare for Challenges and Solutions:

    ○ "Anticipate potential challenges in the deployment of [Selected AI Tool] and propose practical solutions."

5. Finalize and Share Implementation Plans:

    ○ "Finalize the implementation plan for [Selected AI Tool] and prepare a summary to share with stakeholders for feedback."

Activity 3: Reflective Analysis and Feedback Gathering

Tools & Materials Needed:

- Feedback surveys or interview questions

- Data collection and analysis tools

- Guidelines for reflective analysis

Time Needed: Ongoing, with a designated review session after the pilot

Outcome: Valuable feedback and insights from the pilot implementation of the AI tool, informing future technology integration decisions.

Instructions:

1. Conduct Pilot and Collect Data:

    ○ "Utilize [Selected AI Tool] in the educational setting as per the implementation plan and systematically collect data on its usage and effectiveness."

2. Gather User Feedback:

○ "Distribute feedback surveys regarding [Selected AI Tool] to gather insights on user satisfaction and areas for improvement."

3. Analyze Feedback and Reflect on Experience:

○ "Analyze the collected feedback on [Selected AI Tool] and reflect on the tool's impact on teaching and learning processes."

By incorporating these AI prompts, participants have a structured guide to follow, which helps streamline the process of evaluating, selecting, and implementing AI tools in an educational context.

9.3 Customizing AI Solutions for Educational Needs

In the realm of education, the ability to customize AI tools to meet the unique needs of each classroom or administrative function is invaluable. Personalization ensures that AI solutions are not just generic aids but are tailored to enhance specific educational processes, address particular learning objectives, and resolve unique administrative challenges. Customization allows educators to mold AI technologies in ways that directly support their teaching strategies and administrative tasks, leading to more effective and efficient educational outcomes.

Developing and refining AI prompts is a skill that educators can use to better align AI tools with their educational goals and tasks. By understanding how to manipulate and tailor these prompts, educators can guide AI systems to generate more relevant and useful outputs. This process requires a thoughtful examination of educational needs and objectives, as well as an understanding of the capabilities and limitations of AI technologies. Educators equipped with these skills can more effectively integrate AI into their workflows, leading to enhanced learning environments and streamlined administrative processes.

However, the benefits of personalized AI tools extend beyond mere convenience; they promote a more engaged and individualized learning experience for students. When AI tools are tailored to fit the specific context of a classroom, they can provide support that is attuned to the needs of each student, thereby fostering a more inclusive and adaptive learning environment. As educators customize AI solutions, they not only improve their own efficiency and effectiveness but also enhance the educational journey for their students.

Activity 1: Tailoring AI Prompts for Personalized Learning Experiences

Tools & Materials Needed:

- AI tool capable of generating learning content

- List of different learning objectives and styles present in the classroom

- AI prompt development guide

Time Needed: 3 hours

Outcome: Custom AI prompts that generate learning materials tailored to the diverse needs and styles of students in a classroom.

Instructions:

1. Identify Varied Learning Objectives:

    ○ "List distinct learning objectives for an upcoming unit, categorizing them by student learning styles and needs."

2. Develop Custom AI Prompts:

    ○ "Create AI prompts aimed at generating learning materials that address the specific learning objectives and styles identified, ensuring clarity and specificity."

3. Generate and Review Learning Materials:

    ○ "Input the custom AI prompts into the AI tool to produce diverse learning materials. Evaluate the materials for alignment with the specified learning objectives and styles."

4. Share Materials and Gather Peer Feedback:

    ○ "Share the generated learning materials with peers. Use AI to formulate a feedback collection prompt, focusing on the effectiveness and personalization of the materials."

5. Refine AI Prompts Based on Feedback:

    ○ "Refine your AI prompts based on peer feedback, enhancing their ability to produce even more personalized and effective learning materials."

Activity 2: Customizing AI for Efficient Classroom Management

Tools & Materials Needed:

- Access to an AI-powered classroom management tool

- List of common classroom management challenges

- AI prompt customization guide

Time Needed: 2 hours

Outcome: A set of custom AI prompts designed to address specific classroom management challenges, improving overall classroom efficiency.

Instructions:

1. Catalog Classroom Management Challenges:

   ○ "Identify frequent classroom management challenges and categorize them based on their nature (e.g., behavioral, logistical)."

2. Craft Tailored AI Prompts:

   ○ "Develop AI prompts that specifically address the identified classroom management challenges, ensuring they are actionable and targeted."

3. Implement and Assess AI Solutions:

   ○ "Apply the custom AI prompts in the classroom management tool. Observe and record the effectiveness of the AI-driven interventions."

4. Exchange Experiences and Collect Feedback:

   ○ "Present the implemented AI solutions to peers and use AI to generate prompts for collecting constructive feedback."

5. Optimize AI Prompts and Strategies:

   ○ "Revise your AI prompts and strategies based on peer feedback, aiming for enhanced classroom management and student engagement."

Activity 3: Streamlining Administrative Tasks with Custom AI

Tools & Materials Needed:

- AI tool designed for educational administration

- List of repetitive administrative tasks

- Guide for developing effective AI prompts for administration

Time Needed: 3 hours

Outcome: Customized AI prompts that streamline repetitive administrative tasks, increasing operational efficiency.

Instructions:

1. List Repetitive Administrative Tasks:

   ○ "Compile a list of time-consuming administrative tasks currently handled manually."

2. Formulate AI Assistance Prompts:

- "Create specific AI prompts aimed at automating or simplifying the listed administrative tasks, focusing on reducing time and effort."

3. Test and Evaluate AI Solutions:

- "Implement the custom AI prompts in the administrative AI tool. Monitor the outcomes and assess efficiency gains."

4. Share Results and Solicit Peer Insights:

- "Describe the before and after scenarios of using AI in administrative tasks to peers. Generate AI prompts to facilitate a structured discussion on potential improvements."

5. Refine and Implement Enhanced AI Solutions:

- "Refine your AI administrative solutions based on insights gained from peer discussions. Plan for broader implementation of the optimized AI prompts."

6. Post-Implementation AI Prompt for Educators:

- "Generate an evaluation form focused on measuring the impact of personalized AI solutions on classroom efficiency, student learning outcomes, and administrative effectiveness."

Through these activities, participants can delve deeply into the process of customizing AI tools and prompts, ensuring that the technology serves the specific needs of their educational environment, ultimately leading to more personalized, efficient, and effective educational experiences.

9.4 Navigating Ethical Considerations and Privacy Concerns

Incorporating Artificial Intelligence (AI) into educational practices brings a plethora of advantages, from personalized learning paths to efficient administrative processes. However, the deployment of AI in educational settings also introduces significant ethical considerations and privacy concerns that educators must address. Ethical AI use in education encompasses ensuring data privacy, mitigating biases inherent in AI algorithms, and maintaining transparency in AI-driven decisions. These considerations are pivotal to uphold the trust and safety of students and to foster an equitable and inclusive learning environment.

To navigate these ethical terrains, educators need to adopt best practices for ethical AI use, which include strict adherence to data protection laws, regular audits for AI biases, and clear communication with students and parents about AI tools in use. By doing so, educators not only safeguard students' privacy and rights but also contribute to the development of fair and responsible AI applications in education. This requires continuous learning and adaptation as AI technologies evolve and as new ethical challenges emerge.

Understanding and addressing these ethical concerns are crucial steps in creating a responsible AI implementation strategy in schools. Educators and administrators should be equipped with the knowledge to identify potential ethical pitfalls and the skills to apply best practices in their AI initiatives. This holistic approach ensures that AI tools support educational goals without compromising ethical standards or the welfare of the student community.

Activity 1: Analyzing Ethical Scenarios in AI Implementation

Tools & Materials Needed:

- Scenarios depicting AI use in educational settings

- Checklist of ethical considerations and best practices

- Discussion forum or group meeting space

Time Needed: 2 hours

Outcome: Enhanced understanding of ethical considerations in AI use and developed strategies for addressing potential issues.

Instructions:

1. Review Ethical Scenarios:

   ○ "Examine the provided scenarios where AI is used in educational contexts. Identify potential ethical issues related to data privacy, bias, and transparency."

2. Apply Ethical Considerations Checklist:

   ○ "Use the checklist to assess each scenario systematically. Determine if best practices for ethical AI use are being followed or violated."

3. Discuss and Propose Solutions:

   ○ "Discuss your findings and propose ethical solutions or improvements for each scenario. Consider how these solutions can be applied in real-life educational settings."

4. Summarize Key Insights:

   ○ "Summarize the key insights from the discussions and proposed solutions. Highlight how these can inform ethical AI use in education."

Activity 2: Developing an Ethical AI Use Policy

Tools & Materials Needed:

- Template for an ethical AI use policy

- Examples of ethical issues in AI

- Guidelines for protecting student data and ensuring equitable access

Time Needed: 3 hours

Outcome: A comprehensive policy for ethical AI use tailored to the educational institution's needs.

Instructions:

1. Identify Key Ethical Principles:

   ○ "List key ethical principles that should guide AI use in our educational institution, focusing on student data protection and equitable access."

2. Draft the AI Use Policy:

   ○ "Using the provided template, draft an ethical AI use policy incorporating the identified principles, guidelines for data protection, and measures to ensure equity."

3. Review and Refine the Policy:

   ○ "Critically review and refine the drafted policy. Ensure it addresses common ethical concerns with AI and is understandable to all stakeholders."

4. Plan for Policy Implementation:

   ○ "Develop a plan for implementing the ethical AI use policy, including steps for training staff, informing students and parents, and monitoring compliance."

Activity 3: Creating an AI Ethics Training Module for Educators

Tools & Materials Needed:

- Resources on ethical AI use

- Training module template

- Feedback collection tools (e.g., surveys, feedback forms)

Time Needed: 4 hours

Outcome: An educational training module focused on ethical considerations and best practices in AI use for teachers and staff.

Instructions:

1. Compile AI Ethics Content:

   - "Gather educational content on AI ethics, focusing on areas relevant to educators, such as data privacy, algorithmic bias, and transparency."

2. Design the Training Module:

   - "Using the template, design a training module that incorporates the compiled content, interactive activities, and real-life case studies to illustrate ethical AI use."

3. Implement and Gather Feedback:

   - "Conduct the training module with a group of educators. Use feedback tools to collect participants' opinions on the module's effectiveness and clarity."

4. Refine Module Based on Feedback:

   - "Analyze the feedback received and refine the training module to better address educators' needs and enhance understanding of ethical AI use."

5. Post-Implementation AI Prompt for Educators:

   - "Generate a reflection prompt for educators to assess their understanding and implementation of ethical AI principles following the training module."

By completing these activities, educators will better navigate the ethical landscape of AI in education, equipped with practical strategies and policies to ensure responsible and fair AI use. These exercises foster a culture of ethical awareness and proactive problem-solving, ensuring AI tools are used to enhance educational outcomes while respecting student privacy and equity.

9.5 Staying Current with AI Developments

The field of Artificial Intelligence (AI) is evolving at an unprecedented rate, impacting various sectors, including education. For educators, staying current with the latest developments in AI and educational technology is not just beneficial—it's essential for preparing students for the future and enhancing teaching methodologies.

Continuous learning in AI can help educators understand how these advancements can be applied to improve learning outcomes, personalize student experiences, and streamline administrative tasks. Moreover, it equips educators with the knowledge to critically assess the potential impact of new technologies on ethical, privacy, and social fronts.

Participation in professional networks, online forums, and communities dedicated to AI in education serves as a vital resource for educators aiming to stay informed. These platforms provide opportunities for sharing experiences, discussing challenges, and exploring the application of AI tools in various educational contexts. They can also offer insights into the latest research, emerging tools, and best practices in the field, fostering a collaborative environment for professional growth and learning.

Creating a professional development plan focused on AI advancements enables educators to systematically approach their learning journey. Such a plan should include regular updates on AI developments, structured learning opportunities, and active participation in relevant professional communities. By committing to this plan, educators can ensure they remain at the forefront of educational innovation, thereby enhancing their teaching practice and better supporting their students in an increasingly digital world.

Activity 1: Developing a Personal AI Learning Agenda

Tools & Materials Needed:

- Calendar or planning tool

- List of AI educational resources (journals, websites, online courses)

- Directory of AI-focused educational communities

Time Needed: 3 hours

Outcome: A personalized learning agenda dedicated to ongoing AI development and community engagement.

Instructions:

1. Outline AI Learning Objectives:

   ○ "List specific AI topics or areas within educational technology that I aim to understand better over the next six months."

2. Schedule Regular Learning Sessions:

   ○ "Using my calendar, schedule regular weekly or biweekly sessions dedicated to exploring AI advancements, including reading articles, attending webinars, and completing online courses."

3. Identify and Join AI Educational Communities:

      ◦ "Select at least one AI-focused educational community from the directory and join it with the intention to actively participate in discussions, share experiences, and seek advice."

4. Track Progress and Adjust Plan:

      ◦ "Every month, review my learning progress and experiences within the AI community. Adjust my learning agenda based on new interests or changes in AI technology."

Activity 2: AI Trend Analysis and Sharing Session

Tools & Materials Needed:

- Access to recent AI research and articles

- Digital presentation tools

- Platform for sharing sessions (online forum, team meeting)

Time Needed: 2 hours (plus preparation)

Outcome: An insightful presentation on current AI trends and their implications for education.

Instructions:

1. Research Current AI Trends:

      ◦ "Identify and summarize key trends in AI development from the latest research, focusing on their potential impact on educational practices."

2. Prepare a Digital Presentation:

      ◦ "Create a concise digital presentation highlighting the identified AI trends, their educational implications, and practical applications or considerations for teachers and students."

3. Conduct a Sharing Session:

      ◦ "Host a session to share the presentation with colleagues or within an AI-focused educational community, encouraging discussion and exchange of ideas."

4. Gather Feedback and Insights:

      ◦ "Collect feedback from the session participants on the AI trends presented and discuss how these might influence our educational strategies moving forward."

Activity 3: Implementing AI Tool Exploration Project

Tools & Materials Needed:

- Selection of emerging AI tools for education

- Criteria for evaluating AI tools

- Feedback collection forms

Time Needed: 4 hours (plus ongoing evaluation)

Outcome: Hands-on experience with new AI tools and an evaluative report on their applicability in educational settings.

Instructions:

1. Select AI Tools for Exploration:

   ○ "Choose two or three AI tools that are gaining attention in educational technology and outline the features and potential benefits of each for teaching and learning."

2. Develop Evaluation Criteria:

   ○ "Establish a set of criteria to assess the effectiveness, ease of use, and educational impact of each selected AI tool."

3. Test and Evaluate AI Tools:

   ○ "Implement each AI tool in a classroom or administrative context, gathering data and observations based on the established criteria."

4. Compile Evaluation Reports and Share Findings:

   ○ "Create detailed reports on the exploration and evaluation of each AI tool, sharing findings with colleagues or in an AI-focused educational community for broader insights and discussion."

By completing these activities, educators commit to a path of continuous professional development in the field of AI. They not only stay abreast of technological advancements but also contribute to a culture of innovation and informed technology adoption within their educational communities.

Conclusion: Embracing the Future of Education with AI

As we conclude our journey, it's important to reflect on the ground we've covered and to consider the path ahead. Throughout this book, we've explored the multifaceted role of Artificial Intelligence in the educational landscape, from crafting effective AI prompts and personalizing learning experiences to enhancing classroom interactions and streamlining administrative tasks. We delved into critical thinking and creative expression, navigated ethical considerations, and underscored the importance of continuous professional development in the AI era.

The integration of AI into educational settings is not a fleeting trend but a significant shift in how we approach teaching, learning, and educational management. This evolution presents an opportunity to redefine educational paradigms, making learning more accessible, engaging, and aligned with the demands of the 21st century. However, as we've discussed, this integration should be approached with careful consideration—balancing innovation with ethics, personalization with privacy, and automation with critical human oversight.

Looking Forward:

1. Stay Informed: The field of AI is ever-evolving. Continue to engage with new research, technologies, and educational practices that emerge at the intersection of AI and education. Staying current will enable you to make informed decisions and keep your teaching methodologies and administrative strategies relevant and effective.

2. Foster Collaboration: Share your experiences, successes, and challenges with colleagues, both within and beyond your institution. Collaboration fosters a community of practice that can collectively navigate the complexities of integrating AI into education. Engage in professional networks and online communities focused on AI in education to exchange ideas and resources.

3. Reflect and Adapt: Regularly reflect on your use of AI tools and strategies in educational contexts. Gather feedback from students, peers, and stakeholders to assess the impact of AI on learning outcomes and operational efficiencies. Use this feedback to refine your approaches, ensuring they remain student-centered and aligned with educational goals.

4. Advocate for Ethical AI: As you become more experienced in using AI in educational settings, advocate for policies and practices that prioritize ethical considerations, data privacy, and equity. Educators have a critical role in shaping the discourse around AI in education, ensuring it is used responsibly and for the benefit of all students.

5. Embrace Lifelong Learning: Just as we encourage our students to be lifelong learners, so too should we adopt this mindset. Explore new AI tools, experiment with different approaches, and continually seek to enhance your understanding of how AI can be used to support and enrich education.

In closing, the journey through AI and education is one of discovery, innovation, and adaptation. By embracing AI with a thoughtful, informed, and ethical approach, educators can unlock new possibilities for teaching and learning. Remember, the goal of integrating AI into education is not to replace the human element but to enhance it, allowing educators to focus more on what they do best—inspiring, guiding, and nurturing the minds of the next generation.

Thank you for embarking on this journey. May the insights and activities presented in this book serve as a foundation and inspiration for your continued exploration and application of AI in education. The future of education is bright, and with AI as a tool in our arsenal, we are better equipped to face the challenges and seize the opportunities that lie ahead. Let us move forward with confidence, curiosity, and a commitment to creating engaging, inclusive, and effective educational experiences for all learners.